MW00396442

SCHOLASTIC

NAVIGATING NONFICTION

by Alice Boynton and Wiley Blevins

Property of
Shelton Park Elementary

Credits appear on pages 111–112 which constitute an extension of this copyright page.

Copyright © 2007 by Scholastic Inc. All rights reserved. Published by Scholastic Inc. Printed in the U.S.A.

ISBN-13 978-0-439-78287-6
ISBN-10 0-439-78287-2

SCHOLASTIC and associated logos and designs are trademarks and/or registered trademarks of Scholastic Inc.

1 2 3 4 5 6 7 8 9 10   66   15 14 13 12 11 10 09 08 07

Table of Contents

Reading Nonfiction

Nonfiction gives you information. And it gives you information in many different ways. There's the main article, of course. But there is also added information in photos, captions, labels, and even sidebars. Sometimes there are so many features on the page, you don't know where to begin. Let's see how to navigate a page of nonfiction.

Step 1 **Preview the article to get set for what you will read.** The title, photo, and sidebar clearly show that this article is about a disaster—a volcano erupting. If the photo catches your eye, it's fine to stop and look at it. You can study it more carefully later on.

Step 2 **Read the article.** The **introduction** tells you the main idea of the article. Each **heading** is the main idea of the paragraph that follows it.

Step 3 **Read the added information.** Now's the time to read the sidebar and study the photograph and caption. They tell you more about volcanoes.

Practice Your Skills!

1. Put a check (✔) next to the feature that shows how a volcano erupts.

2. Circle the feature that helps you picture what happened the day of the eruption.

3. Why do you think the author gave this article the title "Nature's Fury"?

PAIR SHARE How did you navigate the article?

NATURE'S FURY

*Hundreds of thousands of people ran for their lives as red-hot **lava** oozed over their city, Goma, Congo, swallowing their homes and businesses whole. "I saw my house go up in flames, so we started running," remembers Eddie, a 12-year-old Congolese boy.*

Fiery Disaster

Eddie is one of about 500,000 Goma residents who ran from the city. The **volcano** that devastated Goma is Mount Nyiragongo (nee-ur-uh-GONG-go), an 11,380-foot-tall mountain that is one of the deadliest volcanoes in Africa. The **eruption** in January 2002 destroyed much of Goma. The city was flattened and burning. Many people had no food or clean water for almost a week.

Rebuilding

After the disaster, the United Nations and other groups brought food, water, and other aid to Goma. Gomans began rebuilding their city right away. Nyiragongo can cover our homes with fire, but it cannot kill our spirit," says Salome Kabasele, 22.

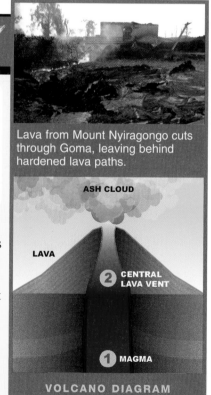

Lava from Mount Nyiragongo cuts through Goma, leaving behind hardened lava paths.

ASH CLOUD

LAVA

2 CENTRAL LAVA VENT

1 MAGMA

VOLCANO DIAGRAM
1. Magma (melted rock) collects in a pool under the surface of the earth.
2. Central lava vents are holes in the volcano through which the hot magma bursts after pressure builds up. Magma becomes lava once it leaves the volcano. Ash, solid rock, and gases also shoot out of the vents.

Practice Your Skills!

Before You Read

Preview the article. Check (✔) the special features it has.

_____ title
_____ sidebar
_____ headings
_____ introduction
_____ map
_____ caption

As You Read

- Did you read the title to learn what the article is about?
  ❏ Yes ❏ No

- Did you use the headings to get you ready to read each section?
  ❏ Yes ❏ No

- Did you study the map?
  ❏ Yes ❏ No

- Explain how you read the article.

After You Read

1. How does the information in the sidebar support the information in the article?

2. In what ways do humans put dogs to good use?

PAIR SHARE Explain what Brian Hare believes about how wolves developed into dogs.

❖A Dog's Life❖ From Wild Wolf to Friendly Fido

Dogs are descendants of wolves. It's believed that domesticated wolves arrived in the Americas by crossing the Bering Land Bridge. The area is now covered by the Bering Strait. (See map.)

How does the family dog know from the look on your face that he or she is in the doghouse?

Believe it or not, your pooch did not learn from experience. There was no need. A recent study has found that dogs have an inborn talent for reading humans, an ability that may explain why they were one of people's first commonly kept pets.

A Survival Skill

Scientists have known for some time that dogs are the descendants of wolves. But they didn't know why some wolves could be **domesticated**, or tamed to live with, by humans.

Researcher Brian Hare says that he has a pretty good idea. He found that dogs are born with a remarkable ability to read people, making a human-dog relationship pretty natural.

Hare believes that wolves developed this people-reading skill as a way of survival. The wolves that became domesticated were the ones that could read humans well enough to find scraps of food. The better those wolves got at reading humans, the more food they found, which increased their chances of survival. Over thousands of years, those wolves turned into today's dogs.

Humans put dogs to good use, too. They used their new sidekicks to help them hunt, for protection, and for companionship.

When and Where

Two other dog studies offer new information on when and where wolves started to buddy up to humans. Researchers compared the genes from ancient dog bones with the genes of today's dogs and wolves. Their findings indicate that the domestication process began some 15,000 years ago in East Asia.

ASIA *Bering Strait* NORTH AMERICA

PACIFIC OCEAN

COMPARISON OF HEAD TRAITS

Head Trait	Wolves	German Shepherds
Ears	• Small to medium • Slightly pointed to rounded tips	• Medium to large • Heavily furred inside
Eyes	• Almond-shaped • Very dark in color	• Almond-shaped • Ringed in black • Shades of brown; never blue
Nose	• Black, with longer, broader snout than most dogs	• Mostly black • Smaller than wolves
Teeth	• Canine teeth are very large, reaching 2 ¼ inches	• Scissor bite • Shorter than 2 ¼ inches

Dogs come in more shapes, sizes, and colors than many other animals. Some researchers have recently concluded that the more than 400 breeds of dog come from just a few wolves that roamed East Asia 15,000 years ago. Domesticated wolves lost some traits because the species didn't need them any more. For example, they no longer had to hunt down other animals for food. Therefore, they no longer needed large muzzles or big teeth. Over thousands of years, dogs developed that had smaller heads and teeth than their original wolf relatives.

On Your Own

Read this article about wolves. Then fill in the missing text features.

Title →

_____

Wolves are wild animals. They survive by hunting and eating large **ungulate** (hooved) animals. They used to be common to most of the Northern Hemisphere. Today, they are found in Canada in the greatest numbers, and are also found in much smaller numbers in Russia, Northern Europe, and some isolated regions in the United States. Most wolves in the United States are in Alaska and extreme northern Minnesota. Some wolves are also in the northern Rocky Mountains.

Heading →

_____

The most distinguishing trait of wolves is their intelligence and social behavior. Wolves are highly social animals, living in family groups called packs. Within the pack there is a ranking structure that keeps the pack organized for purposes of the hunt and the care of the pack.

Wolves are very family oriented. A wolf pack can be most accurately described as a family. This organization meets the needs of wolves. They have survived that way for many thousands of years.

_____
← **Heading**

Wolves communicate in many ways. Body language, gesture, and expression seem to be the primary forms of communication. Wolves do howl, whine, whimper, yip, and sometimes even bark. But when members of the pack are near one another, most communication is nonvocal.

_____
← **Heading**

Wolves depend upon their hunting for survival. Wolves in North America primarily hunt elk. They also hunt deer, moose, bison, mountain goats, antelope, boar, and other similar animals.

_____
_____
_____
← **Describe a possible photo**

_____
_____
_____
← **Write a caption for it**

Reading Nonfiction

Most nonfiction books contain many features. What are these **nonfiction features** and why are they there?

- The chapter **title** tells you what the topic is.

- The **introduction** and **headings** tell you the main ideas.

- **Graphic aids,** such as charts, illustrate facts in the text or add information.

- **Boldface type** signals important words to remember.

- **Pronunciation guides** help you say words you may not have heard before.

Find these features in the article below.

Practice Your Skills!

1. Circle the headings in the article.

2. Put a check (✔) next to the the sidebar diagram.

3. Underline the boldfaced words that are important to understanding the topic.

PAIR SHARE How did you navigate the article?

Dealing With Dollars

Taxes are the biggest source of money that the federal government uses to fund services Americans depend on. Budgeting is key.

Why Budget?

A **budget** is a spending plan. The federal government must decide how many taxpayer dollars will be spent on a variety of goods or services, such as the military, health care, or education. (See *Where the Money Goes.*)

Budgeting is an important skill to learn early on. "It helps you **prioritize** (pry-AHR-uh-tize) where your money is coming from, an when and what to spend it on," says Darien D. Ward, a financial consultant.

Money and You

Each week, Lenzie D., 12, of Illinois, budgets the $20 **allowance** she gets from her parents.

"My parents taught me that you should always save some money and put it in a bank, or somewhere you know you won't take it out and spend it," she said. Lenzie **allocates** portions of her $20 toward clothes or snacks, and as savings.

Learning to budget now can help kids avoid financial disappointments later. "No one can afford to buy everything," says Janet Bodnar, author of *Dollars & Sense for Kids,* "and there are decisions you have to make."

Budgeting has taught Erika L., 13, of South Dakota, the importance of money, and to be mindful of how much things cost.

"I learned that if I wasted my money and bought something I didn't really want, I regretted it," Erika said. "So learning to budget is really helpful!"

Decisions, Decisions: Budgeting, or figuring out how to spend money, can be a difficult job. The government budgets money gained from taxpayers.

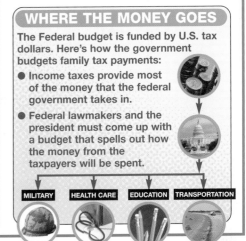
WHERE THE MONEY GOES
The Federal budget is funded by U.S. tax dollars. Here's how the government budgets family tax payments:

- Income taxes provide most of the money that the federal government takes in.

- Federal lawmakers and the president must come up with a budget that spells out how the money from the taxpayers will be spent.

MILITARY   HEALTH CARE   EDUCATION   TRANSPORTATION

Race Against the Clock

Learn to make time by making a schedule

Adrian V., 11, felt like he was in a race he could not win.

After attending school all day, heading off to soccer practice afterward, and then helping out with dinner at home, Adrian would struggle to finish his homework. "I wouldn't have enough time to do my homework, so I'd have to stay up late," Adrian said.

Adrian was forced to hang up his soccer cleats and quit the team after his grades fell.

12 hours a week
Free time to play with the dog or just relax is decreasing.

6 hours a week
Kids today are spending more time on chores, like mowing the lawn, than 20 years ago.

29 1/2 hours a week
Time spent in the classroom, like in this computer class, is a big part of a kid's week.

4 1/2 hours a week
Many kids spend time after school and on weekends playing sports like soccer.

SETTING PRIORITIES

Kids often feel **overwhelmed** as they try to balance homework, household chores, school clubs, baby-sitting, sports practice, music or dance lessons, and even a job.

The key to success during the school year is learning to manage your time—and knowing when to lighten the load, time management experts say. Work with your parents to set priorities. Then make a **schedule** of things to do and stick to it.

"It really lowers one's stress," says Gloria Frender, who has written a number of books on kids and time management. "You don't have to worry about forgetting something."

THE TIME CRUNCH

Kids have significantly less free time than they did 20 years ago. One reason is that more boys and girls are involved in sports. And this doesn't include time spent on music or dance lessons, school clubs, after-school jobs, and chores. Meanwhile, there has been no drop in homework, and for many, the load has increased.

THE PAYOFF

Sticking to a written schedule is a must. Homework is a **priority**.

"I have to prioritize," Adrian says. "I keep a schedule and it helps."

Adrian tackles his homework at the same time each day—immediately after he gets home from school—and makes sure he puts it all in a three-ring binder to stay organized. His stress has dropped, and he feels better. "I'm getting better grades too," he says.

On Your Own

Read the article below. Then complete the activity that follows it.

Getting Your Homework Done

10

It's possible to get your homework done even if you have a busy schedule. Here are some tips to help:

Plan Ahead
1 On Sunday or Monday, write down all your activities for the week in a notebook and then write in homework time each day.

File Your Work
2 Divide a binder into three sections—notes, homework, and tests. Always put papers in their correct spot.

Find the Right Spot
3 Find a quiet area in which to work. Try to find a place where you will not be disturbed.

Stock Up
4 Make sure you have all the tools you need—pens, pencils, paper, and a calculator.

Eat for Energy
5 Your brain needs energy to run. Drink plenty of fluids and eat a healthy snack.

Start Strong
6 Begin with your best subject.

Stay Focused
7 If you start your science homework, finish it before going on to homework in another subject.

Call for Help
8 If you need help, call a classmate. But keep your conversation focused on the homework help you need. Don't start yakking about something else.

Take Five
9 Take a five-minute break when you feel tired. You'll come back to work feeling refreshed and with more energy.

Just Do It!
10 Make homework your top priority and get it done!

What Do You Think ?

An online survey was conducted to determine whether students believe they get too much homework. Here is the response of kids who voted online.

Yes 67%
No 33%

Write three tips of your own.

Tip 1: _____

_____

Tip 2: _____

_____

Tip 3: _____

_____

Practice Your Skills!

Cause/Effect

Before You Read

Vocabulary Use the words to fill in the word map.

destroy   massive
demolish   violent
destructive

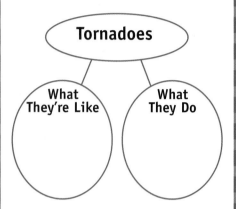

Tornadoes

What They're Like

What They Do

As You Read

Text Structure This article describes the causes and effects of tornadoes. To find an effect, ask yourself, "What happened?" To find the cause, ask yourself "Why did this happen?" Look for clue words, such as *are caused by, causes,* and *as a result.*

Text Feature How do the text features—the title, headings, and added information—help you understand the article?

After You Read

1. What was the effect of the tornado on the Henry family?

2. Study the heading "Surprising but Explainable." What does it tell about weather conditions that cause tornadoes to occur?

3. Why do you think the writer included the information in the sidebar "If a Twister Hits"?

WILD WINDS

Nine-year-old Justin Henry of Mossy Grove, Tennessee, met a force so powerful that it lifted him into midair. It sucked the shoes off his feet. Justin's mom had to grab his ankles to stop the "monster" from taking him too.

Justin had just come face-to-face with a tornado, one of nature's most violent and **destructive** storms. Tornadoes are formed by spinning columns of air that stretch from a storm cloud down to the ground. They can reach speeds of more than 250 mph.

As a result of the tornado, the Henry family's home was shattered, but the family survived. During a tornado, entire communities can be **destroyed.** Tornadoes **demolish** houses, pull trees from the ground, snap telephone poles, and throw cars and trucks several hundred yards through the air. People are injured and even killed. "One day, we had a nice brick house," said Justin's mom, Susan. "The next, we didn't own a toothbrush."

Surprising but Explainable

The deadly weather can catch many Americans off guard. Tornadoes in the United States occur mostly in spring and

THE DAMAGE: A resident looks at a home in Mossy Grove, Tennessee, that was destroyed by a tornado.

summer, and often touch down in "tornado alley," an area between central Texas and Nebraska.

Generally, tornadoes develop one at a time, but sometimes there can be a swarm of them. Why do they happen?

Conditions must be ripe for a tornado outbreak. Often, warm air headed north from the Gulf of Mexico pushes under a **massive** layer of cold air headed east. The collision of cold air and warm air often causes **violent** thunderstorms called supercells. Supercells produce tornadoes. (See *How Tornadoes Form*.)

This type of weather condition is common in the United States, making tornadoes, in general, commonplace. In fact, the United States is the tornado capital of the world. About 1,000 tornadoes touch down each year. They have struck every U.S. state, including Alaska and Hawaii.

Surviving Deadly Weather

Quick thinking helps many people survive deadly twisters. A tornado in Van Wert, Ohio, ripped the top off a movie theater just minutes after a showing. No one was hurt because the theater manager had been warned of the tornado by a tornado alert system. As a result, he told the moviegoers to take shelter in sturdier parts of the building. They all survived.

See *If A Twister Hits . . .* for tips on what to do if a tornado touches down near you.

If a Twister Hits...

Seek Shelter
A basement is best. Rooms without windows, such as closets, are also good shelters.

Protect Yourself
Get under a piece of furniture and/or wrap yourself in a blanket to protect yourself from falling debris. Cover your head and neck with your arms.

Avoid...
cars and mobile homes, if possible. Also, stay out of places with large roofs, such as auditoriums. And don't leave your shelter until the storm has completely passed.

How Tornadoes Form

1 Tornadoes are born of violent thunderstorms called supercells. When warm, wet air pushes through cool, dry air, the cool air pushes the warm air up. High clouds form.

2 Dry air then blows in from another direction. The wind starts to spiral, or spin.

3 As the wind grows stronger, air rushes in from all sides at high speeds. It forms a funnel.

4 As the tornado gets stronger, the funnel stretches and becomes longer. Eventually, it touches the ground.

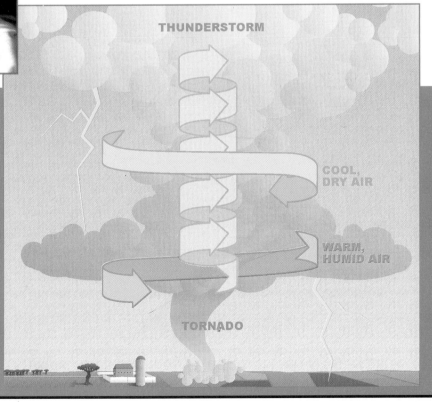

THUNDERSTORM

COOL, DRY AIR

WARM, HUMID AIR

TORNADO

Cause/Effect

Reread "Wild Winds." Fill in the graphic organizer to show how tornadoes form.

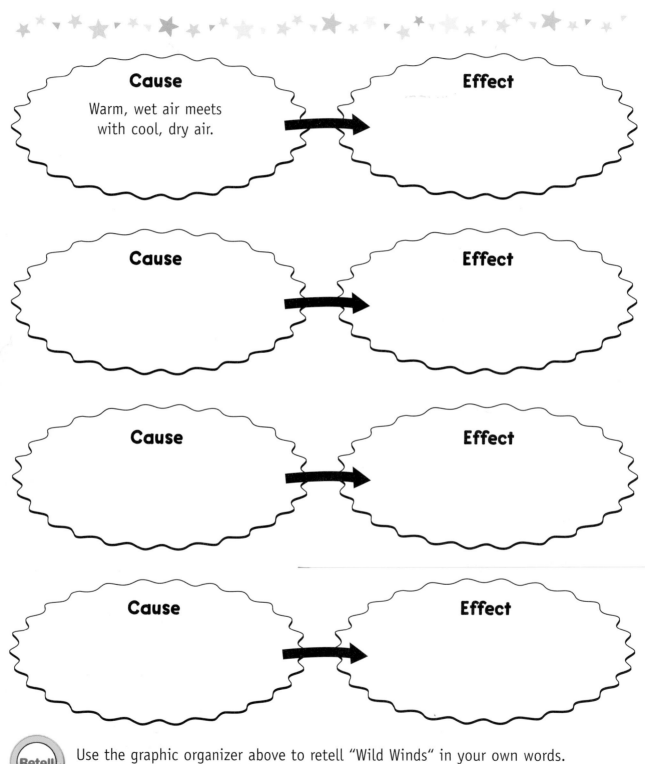

Cause

Warm, wet air meets with cool, dry air.

Effect

Cause

Effect

Cause

Effect

Cause

Effect

Use the graphic organizer above to retell "Wild Winds" in your own words. Include as much information as you can remember.

Writing Frame

Use the information in your graphic organizer to fill in the writing frame.

A tornado begins with a violent thunderstorm. When warm, wet air meets

cool, dry air, the result is that _____

_____

_____ .

Dry air blows in. This causes _____

_____

_____ .

As the wind gets stronger, _____

_____

_____ .

The spinning tornado gets faster. Because of this, _____

_____

_____ .

 Use the writing frame above as a model to write a cause-and-effect paragraph about how an earthquake or hurricane forms. Look in your science textbook if you need facts that will help you fill in the frame.

Special Type

Take a look at a page of nonfiction and what do you see? There are words in **boldface**, in *italics,* and in parentheses ( ). There are words in different fonts, sizes, and even different colors. Why? To make them stand out, so you pay attention to them. They're clues to help you better understand the ideas in the text. Here's how to use them.

Step 1 **The title is treated in a special way that makes it hard to miss.** Read the title to find out the topic of the article. The article below is about finding ancient writing.

Step 2 **The headings are boldfaced. They tell you the main idea of the text that follows.** The two headings in the article are A Vanished Civilization and Written in Stone.

Step 3 **Important vocabulary is in bold or *italic* type.** Important vocabulary about the topic is shown in special type. Be sure you understand what the words mean.

Step 4 **Use the pronunciation guides.** They tell you how to say a word that may be unfamiliar or from another language. Parentheses right after a word sets off the pronunciation. Accented syllables are in capital letters.

Practice Your Skills!

1. Underline the pronunciation guide for the word *hieroglyphics.*

2. Circle the boldfaced word that names an ancient civilization.

3. How can you tell which syllables in *hieroglyphics* are accented?

PAIR SHARE Which other words in the article would you have shown in boldface? For which additional words would you have liked to see pronunciation guides?

ANCIENT WRITING DISCOVERY

A story about an ancient war was recently found written down in a jungle. But the story wasn't written on a piece of paper. This tale was carved into the steps of an ancient pyramid.

A Vanished Civilization

The story tells of a war between two cities in the **Maya** (MY-yuh) Empire, a civilization that disappeared more than 1,000 years ago.

STEP STORY:
These Maya ruins in Tikal, Guatemala, are near the site where ancient writing was found engraved on the steps of a pyramid.

The Maya were American Indian people who created a rich culture in much of Central America and southern Mexico.

The peak time of the Maya civilization existed between the years 250 A.D. and 900 A.D. The Maya created beautiful sculpture and architecture (AR-ki-TEK-chur). They also made great progress in mathematics and developed a calendar.

Written in Stone

The recently discovered writings were found on the stone staircase of a pyramid surrounded by a thick rain forest in Dos Pilas, Guatemala. The story of the war was written in **hieroglyphics** (HYER-uh-GLIF-iks), an alphabet made up of pictures and symbols.

Scientists found the hidden steps after a hurricane ripped a tree covering the stairs from the ground.

Descendants of the Maya still live in Mexico and in Central America today.

Practice Your Skills!

Before You Read

Preview the article. Check (✔) the special features it has.

_____ pronunciations
_____ headings
_____ introduction
_____ boldfaced words
_____ caption

As You Read

• Did you read the title of the article to learn the topic?
❏ Yes ❏ No

• Did you make sure you knew the meaning of boldfaced words?
❏ Yes ❏ No

• Did you use the pronunciation guides?
❏ Yes ❏ No

• Explain how you used the special type in the article.

After You Read

1. What is the syllable system Sequoyah devised called?

2. What motivated Sequoyah to invent a way to write down the Cherokee language?

3. What examples show that Sequoyah knew about other languages and written texts?

PAIR SHARE Why was the Cherokee Phoenix significant?

SEQUOYAH AND THE CHEROKEE

"The children must learn to write and read our language," said Sequoyah (suh-KWOY-uh) in 1809. He wanted his people, the Cherokee, to record their past in writing so they would not forget it. He set himself an incredible task: inventing a way to write the Cherokee language.

The Cherokee

Long ago, many groups of Native Americans lived in the Southeast. The **Cherokee** were among them. They called themselves Aniyuniwiya (an-uh-YEWN-wee-yah), or "first people." By 1770 they numbered about 12,000. The Cherokee originally lived in the area of the Great Lakes. They moved—no one knows exactly when—to an area that is now part of Georgia, Tennessee, North Carolina, and Alabama. One famous Cherokee was Sequoyah, who was also known as George Guess. He accomplished a great thing for his people. He also lived through the difficult changes his people faced.

Cherokee History

Sequoyah was born around 1760 in the Cherokee village of Tuskegee (tus-KEE-gee). This village was located in what is today Tennessee. It was one of more than 40 Cherokee communities in the region.

As a boy Sequoyah was interested in the stories his grandfather and other storytellers told. He was fascinated by the adventures they described.

As he grew older, Sequoyah worried that people might not remember Cherokee history and culture. After talking with Sequoyah, a writer named Jeremiah Evarts said, "Sequoyah had observed white people writing things on paper, and he had seen books; and he knew that what was written down remained and was not forgotten."

Sequoyah's Alphabet

In 1809 Sequoyah started to work on a written language. He thought hard about the words of his language. He realized each word was made up of smaller sounds, or **syllables**. He decided to give a symbol to each of these syllables. This system is called a **syllabary** (SIL-uh-BER-ee). Sequoyah borrowed some of his symbols from the English and Greek alphabets. Yet the sounds they represent are not the same. When he was finished, he had 86 symbols.

Sequoyah's Cherokee syllabary was completed in 1821. Some Cherokee were suspicious of his written language at first. Soon, though, they found how useful it was. By February 1828, the first issue of the *Cherokee Phoenix* rolled off a printing press in Georgia. It was the first newspaper ever printed by Native Americans in one of their own languages.

On Your Own

Read the article below. Think about how the information adds to what you already know about Native American languages.

The Choctaw Code Talkers

Toward the end of World War I, Choctaws, using their native language, helped the United States win key victories against the enemy, Germany.

The Enemy Plan

After winning a bitter battle in France, American soldiers discovered many German communication lines left behind. An American colonel suspected that the Germans had done this on purpose.

He thought the Germans were hoping the Americans would use the phone lines. He knew that the Germans had broken the Americans' secret radio codes. So they wanted to be able to tap in and listen to secret information being sent.

His thinking was correct, but the Germans were in for a surprise.

Choctaw Soldiers Turn the Tide of Battle

As the colonel passed Solomon Lewis and Mitchell Bobb, he heard them conversing in their native Choctaw language. The colonel had an idea!

He gave Lewis and Bobb a message and told them to call it in to headquarters in their native language. At headquarters, Ben Caterby, another Choctaw, translated the message back into English for the commander there. The idea worked. The enemy did not learn the information!

America's Secret Weapon

In each field headquarters messages were translated into the Choctaw language for transmission by radio. That changed the course of the war. The German code experts couldn't decipher the new American code.

The Choctaw Code Talkers Recognition Act was passed by Congress to recognize these brave men's contribution to their country.

Some of the Choctaw code talkers and their commanding officer.

In column 1, write important words you think should be boldfaced. In column 2, write words that might need a pronunciation guide to help the reader. Write the pronunciation in column 3. Use a dictionary if you need help.

① Boldfaced Words	② Words That Need a Pronunciation Guide	③ Pronunciation Guide

Special Type

Nonfiction has many kinds of **special type**—a large colorful title, headings, **boldfaced words,** words in *italics,* and pronunciations (proh-nun-see-AY-shunz). Each kind of special type is a clue to help you figure out the important ideas in the text. Here's how to use them.

Step 1 The title is big and stands out. Read it to find out the topic.

Step 2 The headings are boldfaced. They tell you the main idea of the text that follows.

Step 3 Pay attention to words that are **bold** or *italic.* Be sure you understand their meaning.

Step 4 Use the pronunciation guides. They show how a word is said. Pronunciation guides are shown in parentheses. They follow words that may not be familiar or that are from another language.

Practice Your Skills!

1. (Circle) the boldfaced words.

2. Put an **X** on the pronunciation guides.

3. Underline the phrase that tells why Leonardo isn't what is usually thought of as a mummy.

PAIR SHARE What might paleontologists learn from studying Leonardo?

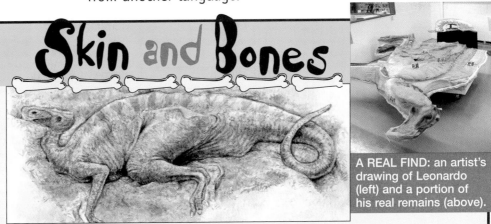

Skin and Bones

A REAL FIND: an artist's drawing of Leonardo (left) and a portion of his real remains (above).

Researchers dig up a dinosaur with its skin still attached.

By studying dinosaur skeletons, **paleontologists** (PALE-ee-uhn-TOL-uh-jists) can get a good idea of how big dinosaurs were, how they moved, and what they ate. But it is much harder to figure out what the creatures really looked like—until now.

A Mummy Dinosaur

A 22-foot-long dinosaur has been dug up in Montana. The find is unusual in that much of the dinosaur's skin, scales, muscle, and foot pads are still intact. The dinosaur, a young **brachylophosaurus** (BRAK-uh-loh-fuh-SOR-uhs), is being called a **mummy** because the tissue on the bones is so well preserved. Even the remains of the creature's last meal—a bunch of plants—were still in its stomach. Researchers named the dinosaur

Leonardo after graffiti of the same name was found near the recovery site.

A Rare Find

Finding skin **fossils** is rare. Researchers believe Leonardo died 77 million years ago at the age of 3 or 4, a teenager in dinosaur years. He is the first teenage brachylophosaurus ever found, and only the fourth dinosaur in the world to have mummy status.

Scientists use the word *mummy* to describe Leonardo, but it is used loosely. Leonardo wasn't wrapped in bandages like actual mummies. Plus, his skin wasn't flesh; it was stone. Researchers believe Leonardo died on a sand dune, where his skin dried out and turned leathery before it could decay.

Journey into the EARTH

Scientists go to great depths to learn more about an amazing cave.

After hiking two miles in the desert heat, cave explorers Hazel Barton and Nancy Holler Aulenbach drip with sweat. But their long, steamy trip is definitely worth the effort. As they lower themselves down on thick ropes into a deep, dark pit, the explorers shine their headlamps on a stunning scene. Spiky **stalactites** (stuh-LAK-tites) hang like icicles from the ceiling, while sparkly crystals coat the walls.

Welcome to Lechuguilla (leh-chuh-GEE-yah) in Carlsbad, New Mexico: the deepest—and most dazzling—cave in the United States.

Deep Down

Scientists say Lechuguilla is about 1,632 feet deep. But new rooms and tunnels are constantly being discovered, causing the cave's measurements to get larger all the time. As explorers travel

For cave explorers like Hazel Barton and Nancy Holler Aulenbach, Lechuguilla is a real treat. The cave has many interesting sites, such as a water-filled chamber called the "Red Lake Room."

further down Lechuguilla's passageways, they find places that no human has ever been. "It's like being the first person on the moon," says Barton. "Your footprints are the first footprints."

The Hole Truth

Although Lechuguilla's caverns and passageways finished forming thousands of years ago, its spectacular **formations** are still growing and changing.

As rainwater drips through holes in Lechuguilla's limestone ceiling, it dissolves rock that's filled with a **mineral** called calcium carbonate (CAL-see-uhm CAR-buhn-ate). As this mineral hardens, it forms into sharp stalactites that hang from the ceiling. A similar thing happens when the water hits the floor, though the effect is different: the mineral forms into **stalagmites** (stuh-LAG-mites) that shoot up like cones from the ground.

"There's an incredible world beneath our feet that hardly anybody knows about," Holler Aulenbach says.

Lechuguilla has many unusual formations. "U-Loops," shown above, grow from the ceiling and resemble stalactites.

On Your Own

Here's an article about creatures that live in a cave in Mexico. After you read the article, fill in the chart to show where special type would help a reader.

Earth's GOOEY Cave Creatures!

Scientist Diana Northrup squeezes into the entrance of Cueva de Villa Luz (KWEH-vah day VEE-ya looz), a cave in Mexico. Her headlamp lights the way. Cave creatures are everywhere. And snottites hang from the ceiling.

Snottites are goopy, sticky cave formations, named after—you guessed it—what comes out of your nose. Unlike stalactites or stalagmites, they are alive. Billions of microbes secrete, or produce, the drippy goo and then call the slime home.

Extreme Life

Scientists call the microbes that make snottites "extremophiles"— creatures that live in places too harsh, or extreme, for humans to live. What's extreme about a snottite's environment? For starters, in a cave, there's no sunlight to provide energy. To get energy, snottites eat a gas called hydrogen sulfide, which bubbles out of the cave's streams. This gas is poisonous to humans and smells like rotten eggs! The snottites give off a waste product that is pure acid, which can burn a human's skin.

To trek through the cave, scientists wear protective gear and carry a gas monitor. It sounds an alarm when the cave's poison-gas levels get dangerously high.

If snottites are so dangerous, why bother studying them? Scientists think snottite microbes have a lot in common with the first life on Earth. Studying snottites might help researchers understand what life was like millions of years ago, or even understand what kind of life could exist on other planets.

In column 1, write important words you think should be boldfaced. In column 2, write additional words that might need a pronunciation guide to help the reader. Write the pronunciation in column 3.

Boldfaced Words	Pronunciation Guide Words	Pronunciation Guide

Compare/Contrast

Before You Read

Vocabulary Read the sentences below. Write **T** if the statement is true or **F** if it's false.

True or False?
1. Children who are **thriving** have difficulty keeping up with their school work. _____
2. Refugees are people who have had a good life in their homeland. _____
3. When you **hire** someone, you offer them a job. _____
4. In an election, the winning candidate gets a **majority** of the votes. _____
5. It doesn't take any time to get **adjusted** to a new school. _____

As You Read

Text Structure This article explains how young immigrants adjust to life in America. It **compares and contrasts** life in their homelands and in the U.S. To keep track of the comparisons, underline phrases that describe how things were in immigrants' homelands. Circle phrases that describe their life in the U.S.

Text Feature How does the special type help you understand the article?

After You Read

1. Describe three great challenges faced by children immigrating to the U.S.

2. Why do most families immigrate to the U.S.?

3. What do you think your greatest challenge would be if your family immigrated to another country? Explain your reasons.

★★

Welcome to

Young immigrants make themselves at home in a whole new land of opportunity.

First Day Jitters

Ten-year-old Dyna Santo had more than a case of the first-day jitters when she started school four years ago.

Dyna could only stare when her teacher and classmates spoke to her. Having just arrived from the Philippines, Dyna spoke no English.

"When I started first grade I was just looking at my teacher because I didn't understand what she was saying, and this made me feel embarrassed and pretty sad," Dyna said.

With the help of a good friend at El Dorado Elementary, her school in San Francisco, California, Dyna was speaking English by the end of the school year. But first-day experiences like Dyna's are more and more common as some 2.4 million **immigrant** children call the United States home and face the **challenges** of moving to a new country—learning English, making new friends, and getting used to life in the United States.

"I remember asking 'Why do we have to move to America?' I had lots of friends in the Philippines and was worried that I wouldn't make friends in America because I didn't know English," Dyna said.

For George Tsereteli, moving to Washington, D.C., was an adventure.

How we got here: Some were explorers.

20,000 B.C.	1492	1585	1607	1619	1620
First people come to North America by walking across a land bridge called the Bering Strait.	Columbus reaches the Americas.	Spanish establish first European settlement in St. Augustine, Florida.	First permanent English colony is established in Jamestown, Virginia.	First time enslaved people are brought to Jamestown, Virginia.	Pilgrims arrive in Massachusetts on the *Mayflower*, seeking religious freedom.

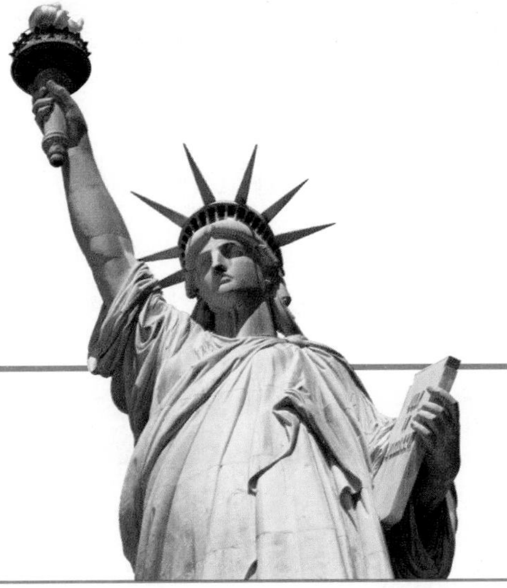

America!

Coming to America

The majority of immigrant children move to the United States to join family already living here. Dyna's mom, grandmother, and many of her cousins were here when Dyna arrived in 1996.

Other children move to the United States because their parents have been hired by American companies. These people are usually skilled workers like engineers, computer programmers, and scientists.

Still other young immigrants arrive in this nation because they have nowhere else to go and can't stay in their home country. These children are forced to leave their homes because of extreme hunger, war, or unfair treatment based on their race, religion, nationality, or political opinions.

When people have to flee their homes because of this kind of mistreatment, they are called **refugees.** Last year, 90,000 refugees were allowed into the United States. The people admitted are from different regions of the world.

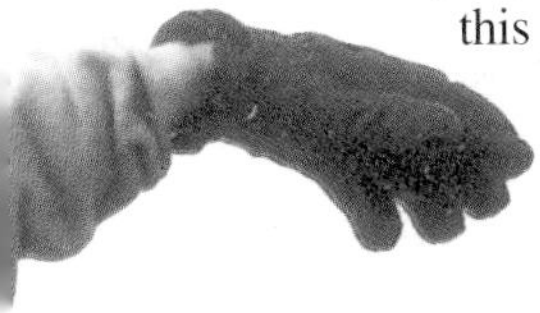

Top 5 countries from which the U.S. welcomes the most immigrants.
Source: Immigrationforum.org

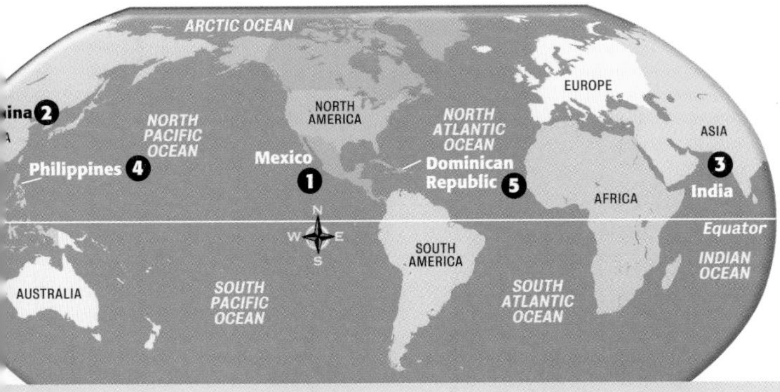
ARCTIC OCEAN
NORTH AMERICA
EUROPE
ASIA
NORTH PACIFIC OCEAN
NORTH ATLANTIC OCEAN
Mexico 1
Dominican Republic 5
India 3
Philippines 4
2
AFRICA
Equator
SOUTH AMERICA
INDIAN OCEAN
AUSTRALIA
SOUTH PACIFIC OCEAN
SOUTH ATLANTIC OCEAN
N
W
E
S

Settling Down

Most newcomers settle in the heavily populated states of New York, Florida, Texas, or, like Dyna and her family, California. But more and more, large groups of immigrants are making their homes in places like Iowa, Louisiana, and Ohio, where jobs are more plentiful.

Eleven-year-old Edgar Silva and his mom moved to Ohio from Mexico when he was 4. They moved to Ohio to join Edgar's dad, who had come to the United States 12 years earlier to find work.

Edgar said learning English was hard at first, but he still is not used to Ohio's cold weather and sometimes misses the warmth of his native Mexico.

A New Beginning

George Tsereteli (SEH-ruh-TEL-ee), 11, and his parents moved to the nation's capital, Washington, D.C., five years ago from Georgia, the former Soviet republic.

"I was excited to move to America, because I wanted to know what it was like. But I was also sad because I was leaving my friends and other family," he said.

Dyna, Edgar, and George agree that the hardest challenge about getting **adjusted** to life in the United States was learning English. But with the support of their classmates, teachers, and family, all three are thriving in their new lives in the United States.

Some came in search of opportunity. Some were forced in chains.

1845	1869	1886	1892	1907	1924	1965	2000
Wave of Irish immigrants come to escape famine.	Japanese come to the West Coast.	Statue of Liberty unveiled.	Ellis Island opens.	One million immigrants pass through Ellis Island in one year.	Laws passed to limit the number of people who can emigrate from certain countries.	Immigration Act of 1965 ends limits on immigrants based on specific country.	These children are from Mexico, the No. 1 country from which immigrants arrive.

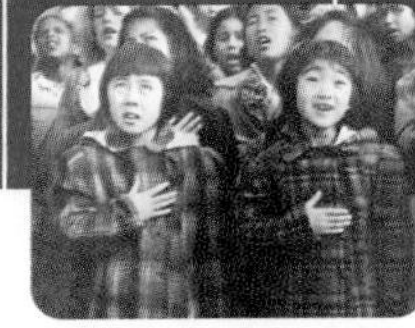

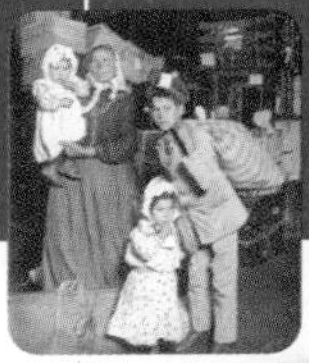

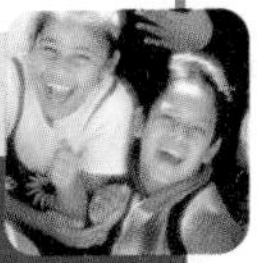

Compare/Contrast

Reread "Welcome to America!" Fill in the graphic organizer to compare and contrast the experiences of Dyna, Edgar, and George.

	Dyna Santo	Edgar Silva	George Tsereteli
Where came from			
Age when came to U.S.			
Where settled in U.S.			
Reasons for coming			
Reactions			
Hardest challenge			

 Use the graphic organizer above to retell "Welcome to America!" in your own words. Include as much information as you can remember.

Writing Frame

Use the information in your graphic organizer to fill in the writing frame.

When Dyna, Edgar, and George came to America, some of the things

they experienced were the same while others were different. All three feel the

same way about what the biggest challenge was. They agree that _____

_____

_____.

However, in many ways Dyna, Edgar, and George had different experiences.

One difference is that _____

_____.

Another difference is that _____.

They are also different because _____

_____,

and _____.

Use the writing frame above as a model to compare and contrast the
experiences of two immigrants you know. Or you may wish to compare
the experiences of immigrants arriving at Ellis Island with those coming
through Angel Island in the early 1900s. Or you may choose to compare two
Native American tribes. Look in your social studies textbook if you need facts
that will help you.

Headings

Most textbooks and magazine articles present information in a way that alerts you to the main ideas in the text. Writers want you to "get it." So, they put in clues to help you.

Step 1 **Read the title to find out who or what the article is about.** The title "Dirt" lets you know the topic.

Step 2 **Read the introduction to learn the main idea of the article.** The introduction tells you why some scientists think dirt and dust may protect people against illnesses.

Step 3 **Read the headings to find out the main idea of each section.** Headings get you ready for what you read.

Step 4 **Look for details to get additional facts.** For example, one detail is the difference between a germ and a virus.

Practice Your Skills!

1. Circle the title.

2. Put an **X** on the headings of this article.

3. Where can you find the main idea of this article?

PAIR SHARE What is the most surprising thing you learned from the article?

DIRT

It sounds wacky, but some scientists think dirt and dust might make kids stronger!

Invader Germs

Alert! Alert! You've just played basketball in the gym and have picked up plenty of new germs and viruses. **Germs** are tiny living organisms that cause disease. **Viruses** are particles that can only live by invading, or infecting, a living cell. When your best friend sneezed all over you (yuck!), he sprayed you with viruses. At least 20 kids touched the ball, covering it with bacteria from their hands. When you touch the ball, and then your eye, bacteria get a free ride into your body. The viruses latch onto cells in your throat, inject their DNA, and make those cells into virus factories. Within hours, the infected cells burst open and thousands of brand new viruses flood your throat. Meanwhile, bacteria are dividing and reproducing in your eye.

The Body Fights Back

But already your body is starting to fight back. An army of white blood cells is always swirling in your bloodstream. Some cells gobble up invaders. Others attack bacteria and viruses with infection-fighting chemicals. White blood cells called killer T cells find and destroy cells infected with viruses.

The Dirt Defense

Some scientists think that dirt acts like a medicine to protect you against allergies and asthma. It may be that the microbes in dirt and dust, and germs from other kids, act like trainers. Those microbes train your helper T cells.

Before You Read
Preview the article. Check (✔) the special features it has.

_____ title
_____ pronunciations
_____ headings
_____ chart
_____ introduction
_____ captions

As You Read
- Did you read the title of the article?
❏ Yes ❏ No

- Did you read all the headings?
❏ Yes ❏ No

- Did you look for details under each heading?
❏ Yes ❏ No

- Explain how you read the article.

After You Read
1. What is the main idea of this article?

2. What information did you learn from the headings?

 PAIR SHARE Which details show that TNX 901 will be an important new drug?

Fighting off Food Allergies

Food allergies can be life threatening. But a new drug may one day help peanut-allergy sufferers to be able to enjoy the snack.

When Kyla Carter was 12, she went to Canobie Lake, an amusement park near her hometown of Kingston, New Hampshire. She splashed down on the log flume and then went to find her mother, who was standing in line to get something to eat. A neon sign warned: French Fries Fried in Peanut Oil.

All of a sudden, Kyla couldn't breathe. "It was very scary," Kyla says. "I didn't know what to do. It's kind of intense. It almost feels like you're choking."

Allergic Reaction

Kyla was having a severe **allergic reaction** to peanuts. She and her mother believe that Kyla inhaled the peanut oil from the amusement park stand. Kyla stopped her reaction by taking a medicine that **combats** allergic reactions.

She may not even need that in the near future. A new drug, called TNX 901, may allow Kyla to tolerate peanuts.

Allergies Are Common

About three million Americans are allergic to peanuts and "tree nuts," such as walnuts, almonds, and cashews. (Peanuts aren't really nuts. They're legumes, like peas are.)

Approximately 30,000 people in the United States go to the emergency room annually for food allergy reactions.

How They Work

An allergy happens when the **immune system** mistakenly believes that a harm<u>less</u> substance is harm<u>ful</u>. When the person eats the food, the immune system tries to protect the body by creating antibodies to that food. The next time the person eats that food, the immune system responds to the "invader" by releasing massive amounts of chemicals. These chemicals trigger allergic symptoms that can make a person ill.

Managing Allergies

The best way to manage allergies is to avoid the food that causes them and to have medication on hand in case an attack happens.

"It's not easy," says Kyla, "But you get used to it."

8 Culprits

About 11 million Americans suffer from food allergies. The foods listed below account for 90 percent of all food-allergy reactions. Keep in mind, though, that a person can be allergic to any food.

PEANUTS

SHELLFISH

MILK

WHEAT

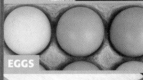
EGGS

SOY

TREE NUT

FISH

SOURCE: The Food Allergy and Anaphylaxis Network

On Your Own

Below is an article about protecting peanut-allergy sufferers. Add a heading that tells the main idea of each paragraph. Then list three important details.

Peanuts Public Enemy Number 1?

For kids with allergies, anything that comes into contact with peanuts can be potentially hazardous. What types of actions are needed to protect peanut-allergy sufferers from harm?

HEADING →　　　　　　　　　　　　　　　　　　　　　　　　　← **HEADING**

The peanut butter and jelly sandwich is an everyday food for some kids. For other kids, the sandwich can be a killer.

"One time, we were on a plane and my daughter was fine," said Janet Weber of her daughter, Emilie, who's allergic to peanuts. "The next minute, she just shut down. She couldn't breathe."

The incident was caused by peanuts somewhere in the cabin of the plane. Just the smell and particles of peanuts in the air put Emilie in a dangerous situation. As a result, Transportation Department officials asked airlines to create peanut-free zones on all U.S. flights.

Some schools are restricting the use of peanuts and peanut butter on campus. Other schools have taken peanut allergies so seriously that they are keeping peanuts and peanut butter out of school altogether. That means no peanut butter and jelly sandwiches allowed!

Scientists estimate that approximately 11 million Americans suffer from true food allergies. "Of all food allergens, peanuts are among the most dangerous," says Dr. Smith, an allergist in Washington, D.C.

Not everyone agrees that keeping peanuts out of schools is the best solution.

"I think that's a little excessive," says Dr. Smith. "But when schools have kids who eat peanut butter sit at separate tables, that works."

Susan Chen's son, Roy, 8, is allergic to peanuts. But his school in Vista, California, does not ban peanuts.

"Roy has to grow up in a world where there are peanuts," his mother said. "So he needs to learn how to deal with it."

Would you want to give up eating peanuts if someone in your school was allergic? What if you were the one who was allergic?

Write three important details from the article.

1. _____

2. _____

3. _____

LESSON 8

Text Feature

Headings

When you read nonfiction, one of the first things you need to know is *What's this article about?* Another thing you need to know is *What's the main idea here?* Writers of nonfiction give you clues that help you answer those questions. Here's how to use those clues.

Step 1 **Read the title to find out the topic.** The article below is about a person who broke barriers.

Step 2 **Read the introduction to find out the main ideas of the article.** This article is about the first African-American man to play baseball in the Major Leagues.

Step 3 **Read the headings to find out the main idea of each section.** Headings get you ready for what you will read.

Step 4 **Look for details to get additional facts.** For example, one detail is that Robinson faced racism.

Practice Your Skills!

1. Underline the sentence that tells about conditions in the South at the time Robinson began playing baseball in the Major Leagues.

2. Circle the headings that tell what it took for Jackie Robinson to break barriers.

PAIR SHARE What did you learn from the article about Jackie Robinson's character?

Breaking Barriers

Jackie Robinson helped solve the problem of injustice in sports.

It may be hard to imagine, but in 1945 there wasn't a single African-American player in professional baseball, football, or basketball. In the South, there were "Jim Crow" laws that set up separate schools, restaurants, hotels, bathrooms, buses, and even water fountains for blacks and whites. But a man named Jackie Robinson was about to take a giant step forward. In 1945, he was the first African-American man to play baseball in the Major Leagues. What did it take to make this happen?

Courage

When Branch Rickey, president of the Brooklyn Dodgers ball club, met with Jackie Robinson, he said that he wanted a "player with guts enough not to fight back." Robinson agreed. While breaking the color barrier in baseball, Jackie had to face racism and insults as he excelled on the field. His courage and talent opened doors in all sports for others to follow.

Determination

On their way to spring training, Jackie and his wife, Rachel, were bumped from three different airplanes. Their seats were given to white people. They finally got on a bus, but they were forced to sit in the back. These were the kinds of **indignities** that African Americans in the South suffered regularly during that time, and Jackie had to practice **determination** to keep working toward his goals.

La Causa

César Chávez's legacy lives on 40 years after La Causa—"the cause"— finally won better treatment for migrant farm workers.

Sometimes at recess, kids run up to Andres Chávez and say, "Hey, I learned about your grandfather today!" Andres, 11, of Tehachapi, California, swells with pride each time it happens.

HIS CHILDHOOD

Andres's grandfather was César Chávez (SEH-zahr CHAH-vez). He was born in 1927 and grew up in Arizona. When he was 10, César and his family moved to California to look for **migrant** farm work.

Migrant farm workers often worked in the hot sun for long hours and lived in very poor housing. They picked crops sprayed with **pesticides** that made them sick. Like all migrant farm workers, the Chávezes earned very little money. Migrant workers were among the poorest paid laborers in America. Sometimes farm owners did not pay them at all.

Migrant farm workers' children attended school, but they changed schools often because the families had to move from place to place. To help support his family, Chávez dropped out of school when he was 14 to work in the fields full-time. He grew increasingly angry at the treatment migrant workers suffered.

THE STRUGGLE

As a young man, Chávez began to study **nonviolent** actions—such as strikes, marches, and boycotts—as a way to fight injustice. In 1962, Chávez and Dolores Huerta, another Mexican American, founded the National Farm Workers Association. The group spoke out for better pay and working conditions from farm owners. But many farm owners, especially grape growers, resisted and continued to treat migrant workers in the same way.

In September 1965, Chávez's group joined a strike against California grape growers. The group urged people to **boycott**, or not buy, California grapes.

Andres Chávez and his younger sister and brother stand in front of a poster of a stamp honoring their grandfather, César Chávez.

Millions of Americans across the nation joined in the grape boycott. Grape growers lost money, which put great pressure on them to settle with the workers.

Finally, in 1970, the grape growers agreed to better pay for migrant workers and to provide health insurance. Chávez died on April 23, 1993. Chávez was awarded the Presidential Medal of Freedom **posthumously** in 1994.

HIS LEGACY

Chávez's grandson, Andres, carries on in his grandfather's footsteps. He attends marches against the use of pesticides on farms and for better wages for farm workers. The hope is that young people everywhere will keep Chávez's legacy alive by continuing to speak out against injustice.

César Chávez picketing for better treatment of migrant workers.

On Your Own

Read the article below. Remember to look for the main ideas and details.

Sojourner Truth, a Northern Slave

Until the early 1800s, slavery existed in some northern states as well as in the South. Sojourner Truth, a slave in New York State, gained her freedom and worked to free others.

Early Life

Sojourner Truth was born in 1797 in a Dutch settlement in upstate New York. Her parents named her Isabella Baumfree. One of 13 children born to slave parents, she spoke only Dutch until she was sold from her family when she was 11 years old. Then she learned to speak English. She never learned to read or write.

She was sold many times and suffered many hardships as a slave. After gaining her freedom in 1828, she settled in New York City.

Accomplishments

In New York City, she began to work with organizations designed to assist women. She later became a traveling preacher and developed a reputation as a powerful speaker. In 1843, Isabella Baumfree changed her name to Sojourner Truth. In New England, she met several famous abolitionists (AB-uh-LISH-uh-nists), including William Lloyd Garrison and Frederick Douglass. She often gave speeches promoting **abolition** and **women's suffrage**. After the Civil War ended, she worked to aid newly freed Southern slaves. Sojourner tried to relocate her fellow blacks to less populated areas, particularly to the Western states. Sojourner urged the government to give them free land in these states and to pay their transportation costs.

Sojourner Truth died in 1883. She was fearless and confident in her determination to help her people. She lived a long and productive life.

 Use the information in the article to complete the outline below.

Topic_____

Early Life

Main Idea_____

Details_____

_____

_____

Accomplishments

Main Idea_____

Details_____

_____

_____

Sequence

Before You Read

Vocabulary Read the sentences below. Answer yes or no.

Yes or No?
1. Water is a liquid that falls from the sky as rain. _____
2. Every fingerprint is unique. _____
3. Enzymes in your stomach help to make you strong. _____
4. Tomatoes need to be taken out of their pods before they are eaten. _____
5. Ice is a solid that forms when water freezes. _____

As You Read

Text Structure This article tells the sequence of steps in making chocolate. To keep track of the major steps in this process, underline each sentence that names a new important step.

Text Feature How do the headings help you retell the article?

After You Read

1. How would you describe the cacao bean when it is harvested?

2. Why does the chocolate maker play an important role in determining the taste of the chocolate he or she makes?

3. Explain the steps in the chocolate-making process in the order in which they happen.

Mmmm...Chocolate!

Your favorite chocolate treat doesn't start out so sweet. Discover how science turns a bitter bean into melt-in-your-mouth chocolate.

CLEAN THE BEANS

As the beans dry, farmers remove any dirt and broken pieces they find.

IT'S LIQUID CHOCOLATE!

To create a unique flavor, chocolate makers mix liquid chocolate with different ingredients and then pour or squirt it into molds.

SOLID AS A BAR

After the liquid chocolate has hardened into a solid bar, it is removed from its mold.

Every year, Americans spend a whopping 4 billion dollars buying treats for their valentines. That's a lot of chocolate hearts!

Though Valentine's Day is a good excuse for a chocolate feast, Americans love this tasty treat year-round. It's no wonder then that chocolate makers spend a lot of time getting chocolate to look and taste just right.

It's a Fruit!

While chocolate may seem like a dream come true, it actually starts out as a fruit that grows on trees. **Cacao** (kuh-KOW) pods—fruits roughly the size and shape of a football—grow on cacao trees in warm regions around the world.

After about six months of soaking up the sun, the pods are ready for harvesting. They are cut down by farmers and then split open. Hidden inside each pod are 20 to 50 purple cacao beans.

The dark beans may look like a tasty treat, but don't pop one in your mouth yet. Raw cacao beans taste **bitter** and are so hard they might chip your tooth! The beans are also covered in a sticky, cream-colored pulp.

Sun Baked

To start the chocolate-making process, farmers prepare the cacao beans for **fermentation** (fur-men-TAY-shun)—a process by which complex sugars are broken down into simpler substances. They scoop out the bean-and-pulp mixture and place it in shallow wooden boxes. Then they cover the boxes with banana leaves and place them out in the sun for about a week. "They stir the mixture around by hand every few days," says Jonathan Haas of the Field Museum of Chicago. The sun's heat—which can raise the temperature of the beans to 125°F—helps **enzymes** (EN-zimes) in the mixture to ferment the beans.

The beans are then dried to keep them from rotting on the long trips to chocolate factories around the world. Farmers lay the beans out to bake in the sun. They check the beans frequently, removing broken ones and cleaning out any dirt. After a few days, the beans have **dehydrated** (dee-HI-dray-tid)—had water removed—and weigh about half as much as they did before. They are then ready to be shipped to factories and made into yummy chocolate.

Hot Chocolate

Ever wonder why different chocolates have different flavors? It's the result of the ingredients added to the chocolate and the method by which the cacao beans are processed. "Every chocolate maker has a secret formula," says Susan Smith of the Chocolate Manufacturers Association.

First, the chocolate makers roast the cacao beans. They place them in a hot oven—at least 250°F—up to two hours. Each company has its own special roasting method.

After the beans have cooled, the shells are removed. What's left behind is a chocolate **solid** called a "nib." About half of this nib is cocoa (koh-koh) butter, a naturally occurring fat.

Large discs or blades are then used to crush the nibs. This motion heats the mixture and melts the cocoa butter into a **liquid**. This liquid is the main ingredient in chocolate.

Secret Recipe

Liquid chocolate may sound like something great to gulp, but it is still bitter tasting. "It takes a little getting used to," says Rose Potts, a food scientist from Blommer Chocolate Company. She tests the liquid's flavor to make sure their product is top notch.

To make a tastier treat, different amounts of liquid chocolate are mixed with **ingredients** like sugar and milk. Food scientists create the perfect recipe by experimenting with various amounts of each ingredient. They also use cacao beans from different parts of the world, because each region produces beans with their own unique taste.

Once the liquid chocolate is mixed just right, chocolate makers pour it into **molds**, where it sits for about 20 minutes at a temperature of 55°F. This allows the chocolate to harden into the shapes you pop into your mouth.

To make sure every batch of chocolate is just right, Potts and her co-workers have to do a lot of nibbling. You might think they get sick of snacking on chocolate. But they all still love it. "We just become more selective about the chocolate we eat."

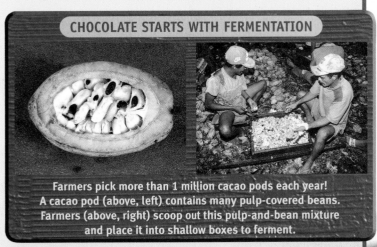

CHOCOLATE STARTS WITH FERMENTATION

Farmers pick more than 1 million cacao pods each year! A cacao pod (above, left) contains many pulp-covered beans. Farmers (above, right) scoop out this pulp-and-bean mixture and place it into shallow boxes to ferment.

Sequence

Reread "Mmmm . . . Chocolate!" Fill in the graphic organizer to show the sequence of steps in making chocolate.

1 Cacao pods are cut down and split open.

2

3

4

5

6

7

8

9

10 Chocolate is removed from molds.

Use the graphic organizer above to retell "Mmmm . . . Chocolate!" in your own words. Include as much information as you can remember.

Writing Frame

Use the information in your graphic organizer to fill in the writing frame.

Making chocolate is a long process. The first step in making chocolate is to

_____.

After that, farmers must _____.

Third, they need to _____.

After that, _____ beans are shipped to factories.

Next, _____.

Following this, _____.

After that, the nibs are melted into a liquid. Next, _____

_____.

Then, _____.

Finally, _____.

The chocolate is ready to eat. YUM!

Use the writing frame above as a model to write a paragraph about the sequence of steps in making something, such as another food item. Look in your social studies or science textbook if you need facts that will help you fill in the frame.

LESSON 10

Diagrams

Nonfiction often contains diagrams to go with the text. A **diagram** is a labeled drawing that shows how something works or how the parts of something are arranged. The diagram helps you "picture" the information in the article and makes it easier to understand.

Step 1 **Read the title to find out what the diagram shows.** The diagram below shows the area under Yellowstone's surface, including the location of a volcano.

Step 2 **Read the labels. They name important parts of the diagram.** The labels identify the layers of Earth and the conditions that can cause an eruption. Follow the arrow from each label to the diagram.

Step 3 **Relate the diagram to the text.** As you read the text, stop and go to the diagram. Find the part of the diagram that the text is discussing. Use the diagram to help you "visualize" the information in the text.

Practice Your Skills!

1. Put an **X** on the location of the volcano's surface opening.

2. Circle the words that name the levels under Earth's surface.

PAIR SHARE Use the diagram to explain what happens during a volcanic explosion.

This National Park Could Explode!

Each year, more than 3 million people visit Yellowstone National Park in Montana to watch as a steaming fountain of hot water bursts from the ground. What many visitors don't know is that Yellowstone is an active volcano and could spurt burning lava—instead of hot water!

Geologists have known for years that the ground under Yellowstone is active. Every day, hot fountains of water called **geysers** (GUY-zers) shoot up from the ground.

A giant bubble of hot melted rock sits under the park. The bubble is from a spike of liquid rock that extends about 1,802 miles down into the Earth's center. Like a straw, the spike draws up hot melted rock from Earth's inner layers.

When hot melted rock fills the bubble, it bursts, causing an **eruption**. The bubble collapses to create a crater. Yellowstone has exploded three times: most recently 640,000 years ago.

Geologists say that another eruption will occur sometime within the next 100,000 years.

Under Yellowstone

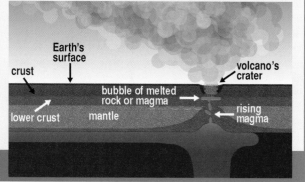

Old Faithful gets its energy from heat deep in the Earth.

34

Practice Your Skills!

Before You Read

Preview the article. Check (✔) the special features it has.

_____ introduction
_____ diagram
_____ labels
_____ captions
_____ pronunciations
_____ boldfaced words

As You Read

- Did you read the title of the diagram?
  ❏ Yes ❏ No

- Did you read each label and connect it to a part of the picture?
  ❏ Yes ❏ No

- Did you stop and think about how the diagram relates to the text?
  ❏ Yes ❏ No

- Explain how you read the diagram.

After You Read

1. Which planet is Pluto's closest neighbor?

2. Where is the Kuiper Belt?

PAIR SHARE How do astronomers add to their knowledge about the universe?

ICE IN SPACE!

HUGE FIND: This illustration shows the huge ice ball that astronomers at California's Palomar Observatory discovered with the 48-inch Oschin Telescope.

A new space discovery gives scientists a different view into our universe.

For the past 72 years, students like you have learned that our solar system is home to nine planets. Now, a giant, dirty ice ball has helped knock one planet—Pluto—off the list. Scientists recently found a large space object orbiting the sun from the outer fringes of our solar system. The Hubble Space Telescope later revealed the object to be 780 miles across. The ice ball—called **Quaoar** (KWAH-oh-ar), after a Native American god—is the largest object found in our solar system since Pluto was first spotted in 1930. The find has sparked excitement among **astronomers**, or people who study outer space. It has also fueled a debate about whether Pluto, also an ice ball, is still truly a planet.

A GREAT DEBATE

A planet is usually defined as a large sphere-shaped object that revolves around the sun and reflects its light. Many agree that Quaoar is too small to be called a planet. Pluto, however, is also very small—one-sixth the size of Earth, and about half the size of Mercury, the next-smallest planet.

Quaoar and Pluto are similar in other ways. Both are located in the Kuiper (KY-per) Belt, both circle the sun, and both are made of ice and rock.

"Quaoar definitely hurts the case for Pluto being a planet," says Mike Brown, who helped discover Quaoar.

According to new guidelines adopted by the International Astronomical Union, Pluto is now a "dwarf planet."

In 2005, NASA **launched** a mission to explore Pluto and its neighbors. It will take the spacecraft, *New Horizons*, about 10 years to reach Pluto!

With the help of telescopes, space probes, and human space travel, we continue to learn just how complex the universe really is.

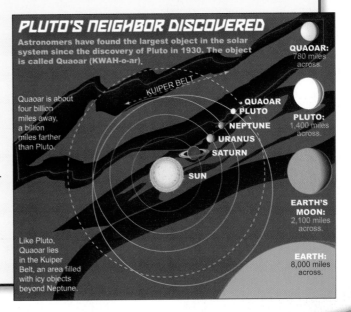

PLUTO'S NEIGHBOR DISCOVERED

Astronomers have found the largest object in the solar system since the discovery of Pluto in 1930. The object is called Quaoar (KWAH-o-ar).

KUIPER BELT

Quaoar is about four billion miles away, a billion miles farther than Pluto.

QUAOAR
PLUTO
NEPTUNE
URANUS
SATURN
SUN

Like Pluto, Quaoar lies in the Kuiper Belt, an area filled with icy objects beyond Neptune.

QUAOAR: 780 miles across.

PLUTO: 1,400 miles across.

EARTH'S MOON: 2,100 miles across.

EARTH: 8,000 miles across.

On Your Own

Label the parts of the diagram that are discussed in the article.

THE SPACE SHUTTLE

Astronauts' exploration of space has taught us to view Earth, ourselves, and the universe in a new way. We realize that Earth is just a tiny "blue marble" in the cosmos.

The space shuttle has made it possible for humans to travel to, live in, and study space. Scientists and engineers designed a craft that could withstand conditions in space and allow humans to journey to and return from the distant parts of our universe. Each part of the shuttle is designed to perform an important function.

❖ The four **payload doors** are large enough to allow instruments, such as telescopes, and cargo to be placed inside the spacecraft.

❖ The **flight deck**, at the front of the shuttle, is designed for the comfort and safety of astronauts traveling on the craft.

❖ The **vertical tail**, a fin at the top rear of the shuttle keeps the craft stable while flying.

❖ The **body flap**, located at the bottom rear of the shuttle, provides a thermal (heat) shield for the engines during re-entry.

❖ The main **propulsion engines**, which are located at the rear of the shuttle, control the movement of the nose of the spacecraft during re-entry.

Diagrams

A **diagram** is a labeled drawing that shows how something works or how the parts of something are arranged. A **flow chart** is a special kind of diagram. It shows the steps in a process in the order they happen. The flow chart helps you "picture" the information and makes it easier to understand. This is how to read a flow chart diagram.

Step 1 **Read the title to find out what the diagram shows.** The diagram below is a flow chart that shows the steps in producing a car.

Step 2 **Read the steps in order.** The numbers and arrows in this flow chart make the steps easy to follow.

Step 3 **Read the explanation for each step. Study the illustration.** Be sure you understand each step before you go on to the next one.

Practice Your Skills!

1. (Circle) the label that tells when the steering wheel is put on.

2. Put an **X** on the label that tells what happens after the body is spray painted.

3. Underline the label that tells the next to the last step.

PAIR SHARE What are some advantages of building cars on an assembly line?

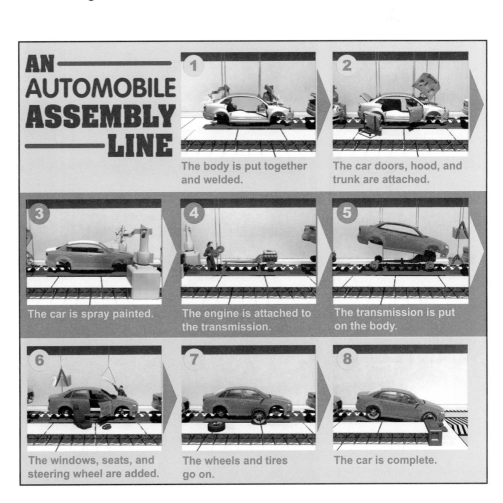

AN AUTOMOBILE ASSEMBLY LINE

1 The body is put together and welded.

2 The car doors, hood, and trunk are attached.

3 The car is spray painted.

4 The engine is attached to the transmission.

5 The transmission is put on the body.

6 The windows, seats, and steering wheel are added.

7 The wheels and tires go on.

8 The car is complete.

Practice Your Skills!

Before You Read

Preview the article. Check (✔) the special features it has.

_____ introduction
_____ arrows
_____ photos
_____ numbered steps
_____ diagram
_____ boldfaced words

As You Read

- Did you read the title of the flow chart diagram?
  ❏ Yes ❏ No

- Did you read each label?
  ❏ Yes ❏ No

- Did you stop to look at the diagram as you read the text?
  ❏ Yes ❏ No

- Explain how you read the diagram.

After You Read

1. Why are all official footballs the same size and shape?

2. In which step is the football blown up?

PAIR SHARE Discuss the steps used in making an official football.

How Footballs Are Made

The first official rules for the game of football, printed in 1894, said only that the ball should be made of leather and hold air. Some balls were short and stubby, while others were long and skinny. To make the game more fair, all official footballs are now the same size and shape.

1 Cutters use a stamp like a cookie cutter to cut the four leather pieces needed to make a football.

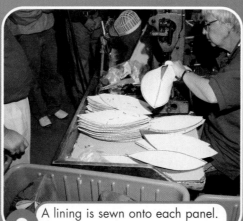

2 A lining is sewn onto each panel. Then the panels are sewn together, inside out. A small opening is left.

3 The football is turned right side out.

4 The bladder, which has a valve so that it can be blown up like a balloon, is pushed in through the opening. Then, the bladder is blown up, stretching the leather and straightening the seams.

5 The football is ready for final lacing with strong cord.

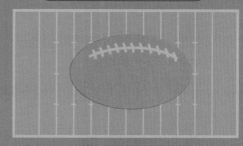

On Your Own

Use the information in the article to complete the flow chart diagram.

The Jeans You Wear!

In 1848, gold was found in California and the Gold Rush began. A big problem with the gold miners' clothes was that the pockets easily tore away from the pants. A man called Jacob Davis had the idea of using metal rivets (fasteners) to hold the pockets and the pants together so that they wouldn't tear. Davis wanted to patent his idea, but he didn't have enough money.

In 1872, Davis offered Levi Strauss, who owned a clothing store, a deal if Strauss would pay for the patent. Strauss accepted, and he started making copper-riveted "waist overalls" (as jeans were called then).

How Jeans Are Made

To make a pair of jeans, a pattern maker first draws a pattern. Then the denim is laid out in layers on a cutting table. After that, a textile cutting machine cuts the separate parts of the jeans. Next, the pieces of denim are sewn together to make the pair of jeans.

Following that, the jeans go to a jeans washing plant where they are washed in very big washing machines. They will be washed for somewhere between 30 minutes and 6 hours to make them look faded.

After the washing process, buttons and rivets are placed on the jeans. Following that, the pants go to the packing room where they are inspected and labels are attached. A typical pair of jeans will have an imitation leather label on the waistband and a wash label with care instructions and size. When all is done, the jeans are packaged and shipped.

How Jeans Are Made

Step 1 ➡ **Step 2** ➡ **Step 3** ➡ **Step 4**

A patternmaker draws a pattern.

Step 5 ➡ **Step 6** ➡ **Step 7** ➡ **Step 8**

LESSON 12

Text Structure

Description

Secrets of a SUPERCOLONY

WATCH OUT, EUROPEAN ANTS! A HUGE COLONY OF ARGENTINE ANTS IS INVADING YOUR TURF.

About 1920, a small **colony** of Argentine ants left their home in South America. They most likely hitched a ride on a ship. Their journey took them thousands of miles away, to Europe. Scientists believe there were as few as 10 ants in the colony.

Today, that colony of ants not only still exists in Europe, but it has grown. It is now a billion-member **supercolony** that stretches 3,600 miles, from the coast of Italy to northwest Spain. That's even longer than the United States is wide!

This supercolony is made up of millions of nests. Normally, ants from different nests fight, but these ants get along. So what's the secret to this supercolony's success? These ants are all **related**. They don't fight because they recognize one another as family.

Smell This!

How do ants recognize their kin? "Through their sense of smell," explains Neil Tsutsui from the University of California, Davis.

Since members of a colony are related, they share many **genes**. For example, they share the gene that determines their **scent**. All ants in a colony have the same smell. This allows them to tell the difference between colony members and outsiders. All outsiders, such as ants that live in nearby nests, smell different. They get attacked.

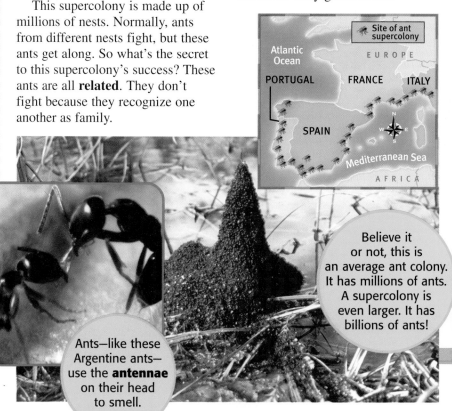

Site of ant supercolony

Atlantic Ocean

EUROPE

PORTUGAL   FRANCE   ITALY

SPAIN

Mediterranean Sea

AFRICA

Ants—like these Argentine ants—use the **antennae** on their head to smell.

Believe it or not, this is an average ant colony. It has millions of ants. A supercolony is even larger. It has billions of ants!

40

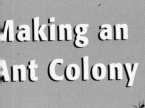

Making an Ant Colony

All in the Family

The Argentine ants expand their supercolony by moving to other nests.

Argentine ants can expand to other nests because they have many queens. Every ant nest needs a queen to lay eggs. Most ant colonies have only one queen. But Argentine ants have up to eight queens for every thousand **worker ants** and **drones**. This allows some of the queens, workers, and drones to leave the old nest and start a new one nearby.

Ants Attack!

The members of the supercolony may get along with one another, but they're nothing but trouble to the ecosystem around them. The supercolony works like a huge invading army against other ants and insects. Experiments have shown Argentines defeating ants six times their size. They even scare away fierce, biting bugs like wasps. They also eat many insects. This affects birds by decreasing the amount of food available to them.

With all the damage the supercolony has caused, scientists are hoping it will one day be stopped. But how? Scientists want to use smell against the ants. They think chemicals from one colony could be collected and sprayed onto the other. That would trick the ants into fighting members of their own colony. Let's hope scientists come up with an answer soon. Argentine ants aren't a problem just in Europe. The tiny critters have invaded every continent on earth, except Antarctica. In fact, if you live in Texas or southern California, one may be marching toward your sugar bowl right now!

1. Arrival of the Queen
After mating with a drone, the queen ant sheds her wings. She then digs a hole in the soil to lay her eggs.

2. Making the Nest
The queen then gathers food, and maintains and defends her nest from predators like spiders and beetles.

3. Laying Eggs
The queen lays hundreds of eggs and tends to them.

4. Caring for Larvae
Wormlike larvae soon hatch. The queen feeds them insects and, sometimes, her own saliva.

5. Metamorphosis
Each larva spins a cocoon around itself and becomes a pupa. Within a few weeks, it changes into an adult. This change is called metamorphosis.

6. Birth of Ants
Most of the pupae that hatch are worker ants. The rest are drones and queens.

7. Males and Females Emerge
When the queens and drones are fully grown, they emerge from the nest. They are now ready to mate.

8. Queen Dies
After about 20 years, the queen that started the colony dies.

eggs

queen

larvae

pupae

Description

Reread "Secrets of a Supercolony." Fill in the description graphic organizer to record facts about Argentine ants.

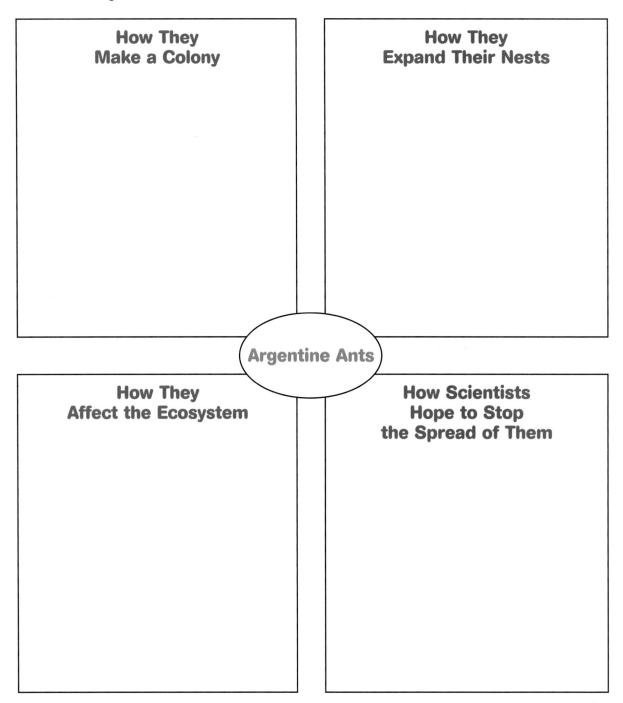

**How They
Make a Colony**

**How They
Expand Their Nests**

Argentine Ants

**How They
Affect the Ecosystem**

**How Scientists
Hope to Stop
the Spread of Them**

Use the graphic organizer above to retell "Secrets of a Supercolony" in your own words. Include as much information as you can remember.

Writing Frame

Use the information in your graphic organizer to fill in the writing frame.

The Argentine ant has many interesting characteristics.

One characteristic is _____

_____

_____

_____ .

Another interesting characteristic is _____

_____

_____

_____ .

Because of these characteristics, the Argentine ant _____

_____

_____

_____ .

 Use the writing frame above as a model to write a paragraph that describes the characteristics of birds, or another interesting animal. Look in your science textbook if you need facts that will help you fill in the frame.

Text Feature

Charts

A **chart** is a special graphic aid, set up like a table, which shows facts about a topic. A chart organizes information in a way that makes it easy to understand.

Step 1 **Read the title and introduction to find out what the chart shows.** The chart below shows facts about endangered and threatened animals and plants.

Step 2 **Read the headings on the columns to learn what information is shown.** The column headings show where endangered and threatened species are found.

Step 3 **Read the information in each row from left to right.** The label for each row names the species included in the chart.

Step 4 **Compare and contrast the information.** One comparison you can make is that mammals are the most endangered animals worldwide.

Practice Your Skills!

1. Underline the title of the chart.

2. Circle the total number of insects that are endangered or threatened.

3. Where are the largest numbers of endangered and threatened flowering plants found?

PAIR SHARE Which species are most at risk? Why do you think this is so?

Endangered and Threatened Species

An endangered species is in immediate peril of becoming extinct, while a threatened one is likely to become endangered without protection.

GROUP	U.S. Endangered	FOREIGN Endangered	U.S. Threatened	FOREIGN Threatened	TOTAL
Mammals 	61	248	8	16	333
Birds 	74	178	15	6	273
Reptiles 	14	65	22	14	115
Amphibians 	9	8	8	1	26
Fishes 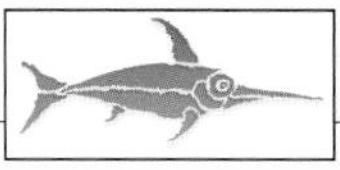	69	11	43	0	123
Insects 	28	4	9	0	41
Flowering Plants 	551	1	137	0	689

Source: U.S. Fish and Wildlife Service

Great horned owls are powerful hunters. Scientists often refer to them as the "tiger" of the bird world. Sight is just one of the things that makes the great horned owl a successful bird of prey.

SIGHT The enormous yellow eyes of the great horned owl let in as much light as possible, allowing the owl to spot its prey in the darkest of nights. It also can see long distances, swooping down from the sky to the ground to capture rabbits, rats, and other small- to medium-size animals on which it feeds.

FLIGHT The great horned owl's wings can span some four feet. It is able to fly quickly and silently, allowing it to sneak up on its prey.

APPETITE Great horned owls are carnivores, or animals that eat meat. They hunt a great variety of animals. In fact, they often smell of skunk, one of the many animals they eat. Other animals on a great horned owl's menu include rabbits, rats, squirrels, and ducks. A great horned owl may take prey two to three times heavier than itself.

YOUNG Mother great horned owls usually lay about two to three eggs at a time. Mom and Dad care for their young for almost a year. Great horned owl nests are usually strewn with partially eaten carcasses provided for the young to eat.

RANGE Great horned owls can be found throughout the Americas.

PREDATORS Virtually none. Sometimes humans can be a cause of death, especially when people hit owls with their cars. Birds preyed upon by great horned owls can sometimes scare them away through a practice called "mobbing." This is where a group of birds will surround the owl, forcing it to fly away.

VOICE The "hoo-hoo" sound that people often associate with owls is made only by the great horned owl.

ANIMAL SPEEDS

In the Air		On Land		In Water	
Animal	Speed (mph)	Animal	Speed (mph)	Animal	Speed (mph)
Peregrine Falcon (dive)	200+	Cheetah	70	Sailfish	68
Spin-Tailed Swift	106	Lion	50	Marlin	50
Duck	53	Rabbit	35	Blue Shark	43
Great Horned Owl	40	Cat (domestic)	30	Sea Lion	25
Bat	30	Chicken	9	Leatherback Turtle	22
Bumblebee	6	Garden Snail	0.03	Sea Horse	0.01

On Your Own

Read the paragraphs below. Then use the information to fill in the chart.

Think about how the chart makes the information easier to read.

Animal Facts

Which animal's baby is called a **kitten** or a **catling**? The answer is a cat, of course. The baby animal weighs 3–4 ounces at birth. The sound of a cat meowing or purring can be quite pleasant. But a **clowder**, a group of cats, can make quite a racket!

The fennec fox is the smallest of all foxes. Its babies, called **pups**, weigh barely one ounce. The sound foxes make is a bark or a yelp. What's a group of fennecs called? They're called either a **skulk** or a **leash**!

A loud roar or growl signals that a mountain lion might be near. Its baby is known as a cub. Although a mountain lion grows quite large, it weighs only one pound at birth! If you should see a **pride** in the wild, watch out! You're looking at a group of mountain lions.

Signets are baby swans. The trumpeter swan weighs only a half pound at birth. Swans can be noisy animals—grunting, hissing, and barking. A group of them, which is called a **herd** or a **bevy**, can sound like an orchestra rehearsing!

Animal Facts

Animal Name	Birth Weight	Baby Name	Group Name	Sounds Made

Charts

A **chart** is a special graphic aid that shows facts about a topic. A chart organizes the information in a way that makes it easy to understand. It shows a lot of information using just a few words.

Step 1 **Read the title and introduction to find out what the chart shows.** The chart below provides facts about several female inventors.

Step 2 **Read the heading on each column.** Each column heading shows the name of an inventor.

Step 3 **Read the information in each row from left to right.** The label for each row names the type of information given in each row.

Step 4 **Compare and contrast the information.**

Practice Your Skills!

1. Circle the row heading that includes facts about the product the person invented.

2. Put an **X** on the year Marion Donovan invented the disposable diaper.

3. Underline the name of the state in which Bette Nesmith Graham was born.

PAIR SHARE Which invention do you think has been the most useful? Why?

AMAZING Inventors

March is Women's History Month. What better way to honor the contributions that women have made than to look at some of the female inventors who have made life in the United States better.

NAME	 MADAME C.J. WALKER	 MARION DONOVAN	 BETTE NESMITH GRAHAM
INVENTION	HAIR POMADE 	DISPOSABLE DIAPER 	CORRECTION FLUID 
YEAR	1905	1950	1954
BIRTH DATE & PLACE	Born 1867 in Delta, Louisiana	Born 1917 in Fort Wayne, Indiana	Born 1924 in San Antonio, Texas

Secret Code of Battle

Native American soldiers used Navajo language to help America win a war.

With bullets whizzing past his head, 17-year-old private Samuel Billison listened closely to his two-way radio. Only Billison and his decoding partner could understand the military orders coming in. Amid smoke and gunfire, he **translated** secret instructions spoken in Navajo, the language of his family.

Billison was a "code talker," part of an **elite** group of about 400 Native American U.S. Marines who fought during World War II.

"We had to go back and forth from translating messages to fighting the war, while running and being shot at," recalls Billison, now 74, of Arizona. "It sounds scary for a 17-year-old, but we were trained not to be afraid. We were Marines."

As a teen, he had helped storm the beaches of Iwo Jima (EE-woe-JEE-mah), a South Pacific island.

Code talkers translated secret messages for the United States during World War II.

A Hollywood studio produced a film about how code talkers went through boot camp, became full-fledged U.S. Marines, and fought bravely in the war.

"The existence of the code talkers was kept secret for 20 years," says Billison. "But people need to know."

In 1942, Philip Johnston, a World War I veteran and engineer raised on a Navajo reservation in the Southwest, convinced the U.S. military to use code talkers.

The Navajo language is not **decipherable** because it is a spoken language, not a written language.

The code talkers were full-fledged U.S. Marines who fought on the front lines while translating the secret codes sent to them by military headquarters.

The code talkers participated in every military assault in the Pacific from 1942 to 1945.

Code talker Samuel Billison holds a U.S. flag in a 1999 parade.

CRACKING THE CODE

Secret Word	Navajo Code Word	Pronunciation
torpedo	fish shell	lo-be-ca
fighter plane	hummingbird	da-he-tih-hi
tank destroyer	tortoise killer	chayda-ga-hi-nail-tsay-di
battleship	whale	lo-tso

On Your Own

The manual alphabet pictured below is used to spell out words with the hands. This is called fingerspelling. Use the chart to practice making the letters of the alphabet. Then figure out the answer to the question.

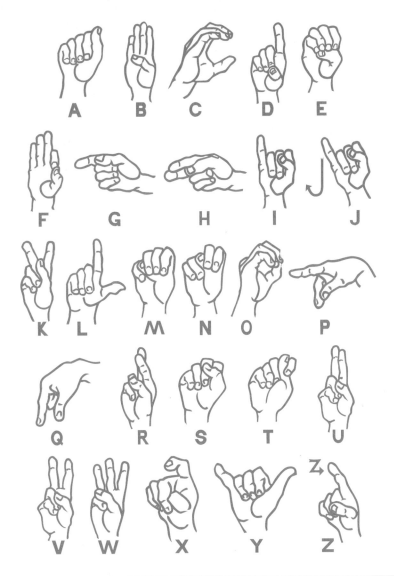

Question

 Turn to a partner. Use the manual alphabet to answer the question above.

Text Structure

Problem/Solution

Before You Read

Vocabulary Read the word pairs. Check **yes** if the words are synonyms; **no** if they are not.

Synonyms—Yes or No?

	YES	NO
dwell live		
species group		
rover ocean animal		
ditch trench		

As You Read

Text Structure This article discusses the **problems** faced by scientists studying ocean life and the **solutions** they invented. To keep track of the problems, underline the words that describe the problems. Circle the words that describe how scientists are overcoming the problems.

Text Feature How does the chart help you understand the article?

After You Read

1. Why do humans know so little about life in the oceans?

2. Study the sidebar. Describe one of the animals that was never seen by humans before the census.

3. Discuss some of the marine-life problems scientists are trying to solve by conducting the census?

Scientists search the seas to find and count all the species that live in the world's oceans.

Creatures of the Deep

OPEN WIDE A coney fish yawns. Yes, fish yawn, too!

Coral reefs like this serve as homes and feeding grounds for many animals.

Underwater Count

All over the world, scientists are diving into the ocean and slogging through sea marshes. They're tagging fish, snapping photos of whales, collecting clams, and sifting through mud.

Why are they doing this? It's all part of the Census (SEN-suhs) of Marine Life, a project aimed at finding, counting, and recording as many species of sea life as possible.

AREAS AND DEPTHS *of the* FOUR MAJOR BODIES OF WATER

Body of Water	Area (square miles)	Average Depth (feet)
Pacific Ocean	64,186,300	12,925
Atlantic Ocean	33,420,000	11,730
Indian Ocean	28,350,500	12,598
Arctic Ocean	5,105,700	3,407

About 1,000 scientists from 70 countries are working on the **census**, which started in 2000 and will continue until 2010. So far, census workers have recorded about 230,000 different species of marine, or saltwater, animals and plants. They have also discovered at least 178 new species of fish, and hundreds of other critters never before known by humans.

Oceans and seas cover about 70% of the Earth's surface but humans still know very little about what lives in them. That's because oceans are so huge and deep. The deepest parts of the ocean are totally dark and have water pressure great enough to crush a person. As a result, humans have been unable to explore deepest ocean areas, where some of the strangest and most interesting creatures dwell.

Diving Deeper

Humans have explored less than five percent of the world's oceans. Now, those working for the Census of Marine Life hope to change that. Using robots, remote-controlled cameras, and deep-sea rovers, the census explorers are searching for life behind every rock, and at the bottom of every ocean trench. They are also scooping up sand and mud to look for creatures too small to be seen by the human eye.

Protecting the Seas

Although Earth's oceans are full of life, many sea creatures are in danger of disappearing. For example, populations of large fish, such as tuna and shark, have dropped by 90% since 1950. The drop is largely due to increased fishing along with rising ocean temperatures. Many countries have passed laws that limit fishing in certain areas and ban the fishing of rare species.

The scientists taking part in the census hope that by understanding and learning more about marine life, they can encourage even more people to preserve the species that live in the oceans.

Census workers are discovering new sea species at a rate of more than two per week. Many of them believe that by the time they finish the census in 2010, they will have recorded as many as 2 million species in all.

Census scientists call this animal an octopod.

DO NOT TOUCH! This scorpionfish is new to science and lives in the Pacific Ocean.

Never Seen by Humans Before!
Some creatures discovered in the census

● **UNKNOWN OCTOPUS** Along with strange-looking jellyfish and worms, scientists found a whole new genus of octopus that they did not know existed. One strange-looking creature, which they nicknamed Dumbo, looks like an octopus, but has wing-like fins that look like elephant ears.

● **PERFECT PARTNERS** A newly discovered species of goby fish lives with a snapping shrimp at its tail. While the goby fish looks out for predators, the shrimp digs a hole that both animals share for shelter.

● **LET'S ROLL!** Rhodoliths are a type of algae that look like toy jacks and roll around the seafloor.

● **OUCH!** A newly found scorpionfish has poisonous spines on its back.

● **SPONGE-BOB'S COUSIN?** A new species of bright-red sponge, called the "rasta sponge," produces chemicals that may be able to treat cancer.

Problem/Solution

Reread "Creatures of the Deep." Fill in the graphic organizer to show the main problem that was discussed, the attempted solutions, and the end result.

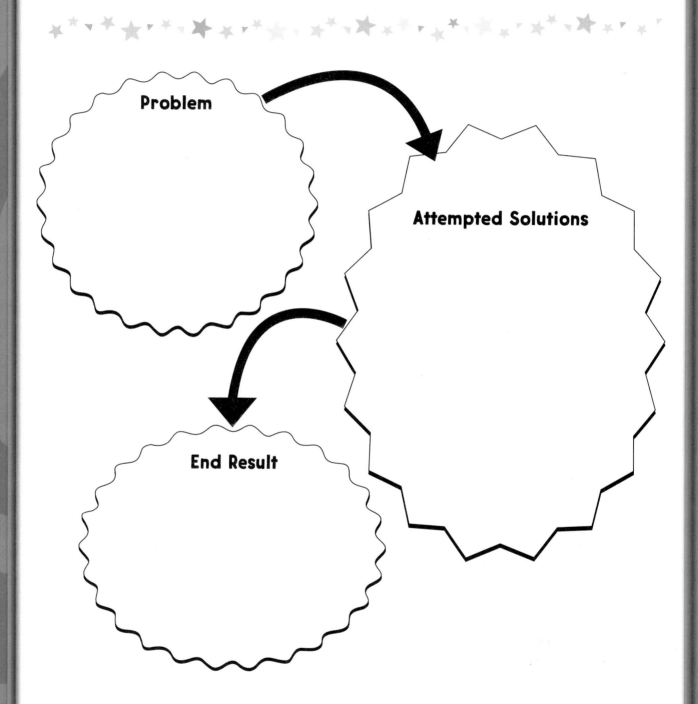

Problem

Attempted Solutions

End Result

Retell Use the graphic organizer above to retell "Creatures of the Deep" in your own words. Include as much information as you can remember.

Writing Frame

Use the information in your graphic organizer to fill in the writing frame.

Many sea creatures are in danger of disappearing. This problem

occurred because _____

_____

_____

_____

_____.

To help solve this problem, scientists _____

_____

_____

_____

_____.

The result is that scientists hope the census will help people better

understand and protect ocean plants and animals.

 Use the writing frame above as a model to write a paragraph about how other endangered animals or plants are being saved. Look in your science textbook if you need facts that will help you fill in the frame.

Photos & Captions

Nonfiction usually contains eye-catching photographs. Sometimes they show what is discussed in the text, so that you can better picture the information. Other times, the photos add to what is in the text, so that you learn something new.

A caption explains what the photo shows. But a caption may also add new information that is not in the text.

Step 1 **Look carefully at the photographs.** Study the details in each photo. Make a mental list of what you see. Keep looking a little longer. If you notice something new, add it to your mental list.

Step 2 **If there is more than one photograph, compare them.** Look for what is similar and what is different.

Step 3 **Read the captions.** Look for information about the topic— not just what is pictured, but also what is additional.

Practice Your Skills!

1. Underline the caption that contradicts what some people believe about bats.

2. What new information did you learn about the pallid bat from the photo?

PAIR SHARE Choose one photo and describe what you see. How is what you see the same as what your partner sees? How is it different?

BATS of the WORLD

The world has 975 different bat species. Here are just a few of them.

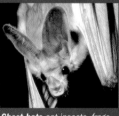
Ghost bats eat insects, frogs, reptiles, birds, and even other bats.

Australian Ghost Bat
Ghost bats live in Northern Australia. They get their names from their white bodies and silent flying.

Despite what some people think, vampire bats feed off cattle, not people.

Pallid Bat
Pallid bats live in most of North America and have good sight. Thanks to their large ears, pallid bats have excellent hearing. They can even hear insects walking on the ground.

This pallid bat has just caught a scorpion spider for dinner.

Vampire Bat
Vampire bats live in Latin America. They suck the blood of their prey by sinking their front teeth into the skin and lapping up the blood with their grooved tongues.

Practice Your Skills!

Before You Read

Preview the article. Check (✔) the special features it has.

_____ title
_____ chart
_____ headings
_____ captions
_____ map
_____ photos

As You Read

• Did you study the details in the photographs?
❏ Yes ❏ No

• Did you read the captions carefully?
❏ Yes ❏ No

• Did you note the information the captions added to the article?
❏ Yes ❏ No

• Explain what you learned from the photos and captions.

After You Read

1. What information does the caption under the picture of Mexican free-tailed bats add to the article?

2. Compare the purpose of the Wild Sanctuary to the purpose of Bat World.

3. From looking at the photo of the bat Lollar helped at Bat World, how would you describe the animal?

PAIR SHARE Why might the author have written this article?

Bat Buddy

Read about one woman's crusade to protect bats!

This is one of the many bats that Amanda Lollar helped at Bat World.

Living with more than a hundred bats may seem batty, but Amanda Lollar doesn't think so. She's made caring for them her life's work.

Lollar started two centers for bats. One is Bat World for **injured** bats. And the other is the Wild Sanctuary, a **shelter** for healthy bats.

"Bats are probably the most misunderstood animal on the planet," Lollar says.

A Change of Heart

But Lollar hasn't always liked bats. Like many people, she used to think bats were scary creatures.

While caring for an injured bat, Lollar began researching the winged mammals and realized how misunderstood they were.

For example, Lollar learned that bats do not drink human blood. Vampire bats are the only bats that suck blood, and they mainly prey on farm animals, not humans. She also learned that bats don't attack people, and they are not full of disease. In fact,

This is one of the injured bats that Amanda nursed back to health. It is in a cage that seems like the bat's natural habitat with plants and trees that would be in the wild.

she discovered that bats help humans by eating millions of mosquitoes and crop-eating bugs.

Bats in Need

Bats have been helping humans for centuries, but now bats need the help of humans. Today, bats are the most-endangered land mammal in North America.

Many bat species are **endangered** because construction often destroys their homes, leaving them with no place to live.

"As many as 30,000 bats live in the Wild Sanctuary," says Lollar. The bats come and go as they please.

Injured bats are brought to Bat World. Lollar nurses the bats back to health and releases most of them back into the wild. But some stay because they can no longer survive on their own.

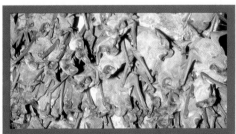

These Mexican free-tailed bats are hanging around trying to get some sleep. These bats can be found in the southwestern United States.

On Your Own

Study the photographs. List the details you notice in each one. Then read the captions and underline additional information beyond what is pictured in each photo.

At one time, people thought bats were birds without feathers. That's because bats can fly. We now know that bats are mammals. They are warm-blooded, they nurse their babies, and they have fur.

Details From Photograph

_____

_____

_____

Details From Caption

_____

_____

_____

Bats are special mammals because they are the only ones that fly. Flying squirrels are mammals, too, but they don't really fly. They jump from a high tree and glide through the air like a kite. However, bats flap their wings and fly the way a bird does.

Details From Photograph

_____

_____

_____

Details From Caption

_____

_____

_____

Text Feature

Photos & Captions

A **photograph** is a kind of primary source. It shows you details about people, places, and events in a particular time period. For example, photographs of Civil War soldiers help you "see" what being a soldier was like in the 1860s. Or a photo can show something that exists today. And it might even be something that you have never seen before. A **caption** explains what is shown in the photo and often adds new information that is not in the text.

Step 1 **Look carefully at the photos. They can add to what you learn from the text.** Look at the photos more than once. Try to notice something new each time.

Step 2 **Make comparisons.** Ask yourself, "How is what I see in the photo the same as something else I know about? How is it different?"

Step 3 **Read the captions.** They often add new information.

Practice Your Skills!

1. Circle the photo that shows what the ice hotel has in common with other hotels.

2. Underline the caption that tells about another Ice Hotel.

PAIR SHARE In what ways is this hotel similar and different from most other hotels?

All Snowed Inn

A guest reads at the Ice Hotel in Canada.

North America's first Ice Hotel treats guests to a cool adventure.

A hotel in Canada is the coolest vacation spot—but check it out before it melts.

The Ice Hotel, near Quebec City, Canada, is made entirely of ice. Everything—from the walls and floors to the beds, desks, and lamps—is crafted out of ice. The electrical wiring is coated with a special plastic to keep it dry.

Nearly 4,500 tons of snow and 250 tons of ice were shoveled, chiseled, stacked, and packed to create the Ice Hotel.

It will melt by early April as spring arrives. The hotel will be rebuilt at the start of winter.

Snow blankets the floors of the hotel. Chairs and tables are carved out of large pieces of ice. Even the beds are made of ice slabs covered with reindeer skins.

People from all over the world have already reserved rooms at the chilly hotel. "It's so beautiful," says a guest. "You feel like you're in a fairy tale."

The hotel in Canada is modeled after Sweden's Ice Hotel. All the furniture in both hotels is made of ice, including the chairs, lamps, and fireplace.

Practice Your Skills!

Before You Read

Preview the article. Check (✔) the features it has.

_____ title
_____ sidebar
_____ pronunciations
_____ photos
_____ captions
_____ boldfaced words

As You Read

• Did you look at the photographs?
❏ Yes ❏ No

• Did you read the captions?
❏ Yes ❏ No

• Did you note details in the photos that add information to the text?
❏ Yes ❏ No

After You Read

1. What information did you learn from the photo captions?

2. Which facts would you use to show that Cameron and Isaiah feel it is important to make people who are not Native Americans aware of their culture?

PAIR SHARE In what ways are playing football and being a grass dancer similar and different? Support your answer with information from the text.

DANCING WITH PRIDE

Brothers Isaiah and Cameron Poorbear use the beauty of dance to celebrate their Native American heritage.

Sixth grader Isaiah Poorbear and his younger brother Cameron love putting on their pads and helmets and hitting the football field.

Isaiah and Cameron also love to dance. It is their way of honoring their Native American culture and keeping it alive.

A History in Dance

Cameron and Isaiah are Oglala Lakota (also known as Sioux). They and their parents frequently attend Native American **powwows**, or large social gatherings. Isaiah, who is 12 years old, has been performing the Grass Dance at powwows throughout the West since he was 9. Cameron, 10, started performing the dance with his brother last year.

Dance is a big part of Native American culture. Centuries ago, Native Americans danced to honor warriors as they prepared to hunt or do battle. They also danced for many other **ceremonies**, including a young person's initiation into the tribe.

Today, Native Americans dance to celebrate and reaffirm their shared

The brothers play football for their local Boys & Girls Club.

heritage and **tradition**. Important to this tradition are the elaborate costumes dancers wear and the drum beats they dance to. Drummers spend years perfecting their craft.

Grass dancers wear long, thick fringes made of yarn or ribbon that cover a dancer from shoulder to ankle. The outfit represents grass flowing on a prairie, according to the boys. They learned the Grass Dance by watching older people perform it.

Sharing Culture

Isaiah says he wants to play football or hockey when he grows up, as well as "travel the world teaching others about my heritage."

The powwows are one way to do this. The boys travel to powwows across the West from South Dakota to New Mexico. The big powwows draw thousands of Native Americans, as well as non–Native Americans who come to watch the dancing.

Spirited Kids

Cameron and Isaiah are happy that people who are not Native American come to the powwows. They want others to benefit from their culture.

"We know that we are making people feel good inside while they watch us dance," they say.

Cameron Poorbear (left) and his brother Isaiah in their Grass Dance dress.

On Your Own

The photos below show Native Americans who lived in the northern Great Plains from the late 1800s to early 1900s. Look at the photographs and read the captions. Decide which caption belongs with which picture. Write the number of the caption below the picture.

Caption #_____

Caption #_____

Caption #_____

Captions

1. This Native American is wearing traditional Lakota dance attire, complete with dance bells and feather headdress. He is in front of a U.S. military tent.

2. American flags serve as window coverings on the building behind this Native American woman. An old saddle and blanket can be seen at the left.

3. Traditional dance regalia includes moccasins, a shirt appropriate for a powwow, and a breastplate. The dancer's belt is draped across the saddle horn.

What information would you need in order to be able to write a caption for this photo? Make a list.

_____

_____

_____

_____

_____

Text Structure

Compare/Contrast

Before You Read

Vocabulary Use each word below to complete the sentences in the chart.

repellent   submerged
douse   scour   snout

What's the Relationship?
All is to **none** as **attractive** is to _____.
Foot is to **hoof** as **nose** is to _____.
All is to **every** as **sunken** is to _____.
Search is to **seek** as **scrub** is to _____.
Other is to **same** as **dry off** is to _____.

As You Read

Text Structure This article **compares** and **contrasts** the physical characteristics of crocodiles and alligators.

Text Feature How do the photographs and captions help you understand the article?

After You Read

1. What characteristics do both crocodiles and alligators have?

2. How did Daphne Soares first discover that a "beard" helps crocodilians catch their prey?

3. Which examples from the text show that Daphne is a careful researcher?

Croc Chasers

Follow crocs into the wilderness to see how they find their food.

Sharp teeth and powerful jaws help this crocodile hold onto its prey.

It's late at night and pitch-dark in a brown, muddy swamp. A long, scaly crocodile with leathery skin lazes half-submerged in the murky waters. It's awaiting its next meal. Suddenly, a frog leaps through the air to perch on a delicate lily

What's so different about reptiles?

They're *cold-blooded* animals—their body temperatures depend on the temperature outside. They usually lay their young in eggs.

pad. At lightning-fast speed, the croc lunges toward the unsuspecting frog. CHOMP! The crocodile's fierce jaws and razor-sharp teeth lock onto its prey.

Sixth Sense

Until recently, scientists thought that crocs and alligators needed amazing eyesight to catch their prey at night. They thought the reptiles relied on their eyes to snatch food. But Daphne Soares, a researcher from the University of Maryland,

A baby crocodilian in its marshy habitat.

has discovered otherwise. She found that, with the help of a "beard" of tiny, bumpy spots along their jaws, crocodilians (a reptile group that includes alligators and crocodiles) can not only see—but also feel—when supper lands in front of them.

While studying crocodilians, Daphne Soares noticed this tiny beard on a gator. She discovered that the spots help these reptiles sense prey in the water.

Lassoing Gators

Daphne first noticed the crocodilians' bumpy beards last year. She and two other researchers doused (dowst) themselves in mosquito repellent. Then they scoured the Louisiana landscape in search of crocodilians.

After trudging through muddy waters, they spotted a six-foot-long alligator. They lassoed the gator out of the waters to bring back to Daphne's lab for a look. But Daphne's investigation began before she even reached the lab.

She and the other researchers loaded the alligator into the back of her pickup truck. That's when she noticed the gator's bumps.

"I was looking at his jaw," Daphne says. "And I thought, 'I wonder what those little spots are for?'"

Telltale Test

Daphne solved the mystery with an experiment: Back at her lab, she covered the eyes, ears, and noses of some young gators and placed them in a pool of water. Then, she gently dripped water droplets on the pool's surface. The gators reacted to the drops instantly, lunging and snapping at what they thought would be a tasty meal.

Next, Daphne repeated the experiment. This time, she covered the bumps on the alligators' jaws. The alligators didn't react at all to the water droplets. Daphne concluded that when an animal hits the water in which an alligator or crocodile lurks, it sends a ripple through the water. The crocodilian's beard feels the ripple and signals a message to its brain. The brain quickly figures out where the ripple came from. Then the hungry reptile lunges toward its prey with a deadly, jaw-smashing crunch.

Croc or Gator? When in doubt, check the snout.

Croc
• Has a narrow snout.
• Its fourth tooth (on both sides) sticks out of its closed mouth.
• Is olive or gray with black spots.

Gator
• Has a rounded snout.
• Its fourth tooth (on both sides) does not stick out of its mouth.
• Is all black.

Compare/Contrast

Reread "Croc Chasers." Fill in the graphic organizer with details that compare and contrast the characteristics of crocodiles and alligators.

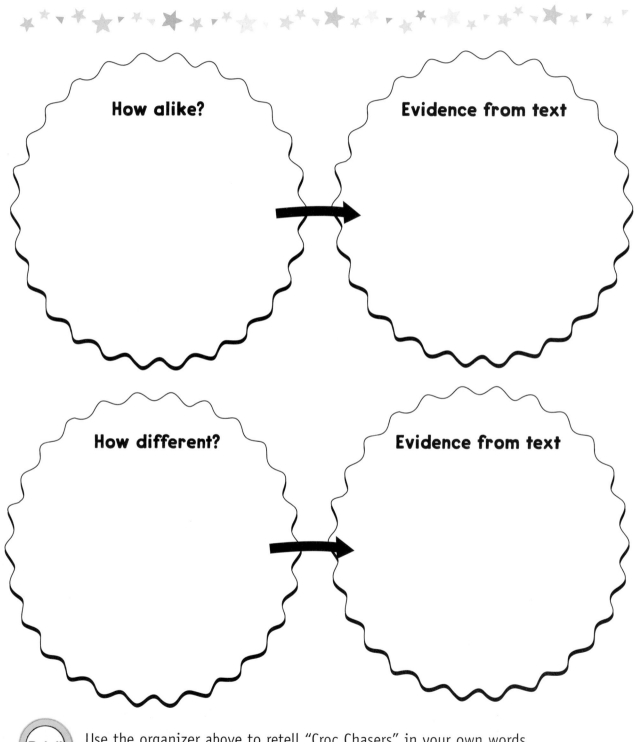

How alike?

Evidence from text

How different?

Evidence from text

Use the organizer above to retell "Croc Chasers" in your own words. Include as much information as you can remember.

Writing Frame

Use the information in your graphic organizer to fill in the writing frame.

Alligators and crocodiles are similar in many ways. They are alike because

_____.They are also alike because

_____.

In addition, they both _____.

In some ways, however, _____ and _____

_____ are different. They are different because _____

_____.

They are also different because _____

_____.

Another difference is _____

_____.

So, _____ and _____ are alike in

some ways and different in others.

 Use the writing frame above as a model to compare and contrast two mammals, two kinds of trees, or two metals. Look in your science textbook if you need facts that will help you fill in the frame.

LESSON 19

Text Feature

Graphs

The expression "A picture is worth a thousand words" is really true about a graph. A **graph** is a diagram, a kind of picture, that shows numerical information with very few words. It allows you to make comparisons and draw conclusions quickly and easily.

A **line graph** shows changes over time. A **circle graph**, also called a pie graph, shows how the parts of something add up to the whole. A **bar graph** uses bars of different heights to compare amounts. Follow the steps to get the picture.

Step 1 **Read the title to find out what the graph is about.**

Step 2 **Study the labels.** On the **line graph** below, the labels on the left side tell the number of DVD players sold. The labels along the bottom tell the years that the graph covers—1997 to 2004. Trace the line of dots to see the changes.

On the **circle graph** below, labels tell what kids spend money on and the percentage of total money that was spent on each thing. Look at the sizes of the parts to compare them.

Step 3 **Compare facts and figures.** For example, did the number of DVD players sold go up or down? What do kids spend almost the same amounts of money on?

Practice Your Skills!

1. Put an **X** on the year in which DVD sales rose above 10 million.

2. Between which years did DVD sales increase the most? How did you figure it out?

3. On the pie graph, circle the two categories in which kids spend the largest percentage of their money.

PAIR SHARE Based on the information on the line graph, do you predict that DVD player sales will continue to show large increases in future years? Explain your reasons.

Consumer $ales

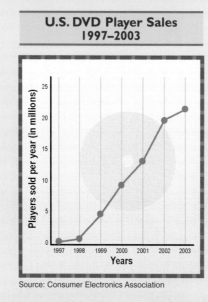

U.S. DVD Player Sales 1997–2003

Source: Consumer Electronics Association

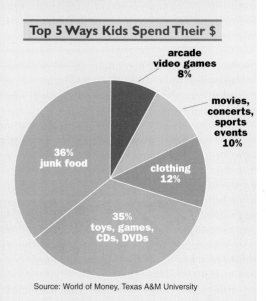

Top 5 Ways Kids Spend Their $

arcade video games 8%

movies, concerts, sports events 10%

36% junk food

clothing 12%

35% toys, games, CDs, DVDs

Source: World of Money, Texas A&M University

64

A REAL EDUCATION IN MONEY

Students learn the power of a dollar in a hands-on program in which they create and manage their own businesses.

Tiffany Medina and Jasmine Sutherland eagerly approach loan officer Vanessa Marrero at the Elmwood Bank. "We have a business and we are trying to get a **loan**," the girls explain.

Tiffany and Jasmine hope to get startup **capital** for their business, T&J Picture Frames. "We make picture frames and sell them," Jasmine says. "We can put a person's name on it, or we can design it any way our customer wants it."

But before Tiffany and Jasmine can get their business off the ground, they need to buy supplies and have enough

COOL CASH
Elmwood students created their own money—the Eagle.

money to pay the 10 employees included in their business plan. They turn to the bank for a loan.

Taking Responsibility

Vanessa looks over their application and asks a few questions. She speaks with her manager, and then she returns with good news for the girls: "I brought your application to my boss, and he approved your loan." Vanessa writes a check for the girls and sends them on their way.

In return for the loan, Tiffany and Jasmine will **repay** the bank a 5 percent **fee** in addition to what they borrowed.

Learning by Doing

Tiffany and Jasmine's experience is similar to that of many business owners who apply for a bank loan. But all these business owners are kids, students at Elmwood Elementary School in New York. They produce real **products** and **services**, but instead of dollars they use their own currency—Eagles. It's all part of a special program at Elmwood Elementary called MicroSociety. The program, which is in about 200 schools across the country, teaches kids about money matters by letting them set up and run their own businesses at school.

Elmwood students run more than 20 different businesses, including a T-shirt-making operation and the selling of chocolate candy.

The Life of a $ Bill

How long has that $1 bill been living in your pocket? Of all the different bills of U.S. currency, $1 bills have the shortest life span. After the bills spend 18 months in circulation, the Bureau of Engraving and Printing collects them from banks and recycles the paper to make new bills. Compare the life span of a $1 bill with the average life spans of other bills.

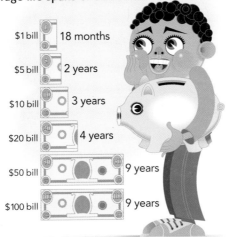

$1 bill — 18 months
$5 bill — 2 years
$10 bill — 3 years
$20 bill — 4 years
$50 bill — 9 years
$100 bill — 9 years

Source: Federal Reserve System; Bureau of Engraving and Printing

On Your Own

Below is an article about kids' average weekly allowances. Use the information to complete the bar graph. Here's how:

- Provide a title for the graph.

- Label the left side with the average allowance per week. Label the bottom with the kids' ages.

- Fill in the bars to show the average weekly allowance for kids of each age.

$ $ $ KIDS' MONEY $ $

Many kids in America receive an **allowance**, or a certain amount of money each week from their family. Allowances often help kids learn to manage money and make responsible spending and saving decisions.

At age 8, the average weekly allowance is $4.50. At age 9, kids' average allowance is $5.50. By the time most kids reach age 10, their family, on average, gives them $7.50. At 11, kids' average allowance is $8.00. Most 12-year-olds get $9.50. The surprising news is that, on average, 13-year-olds only get $9.00.

(graph title) _____

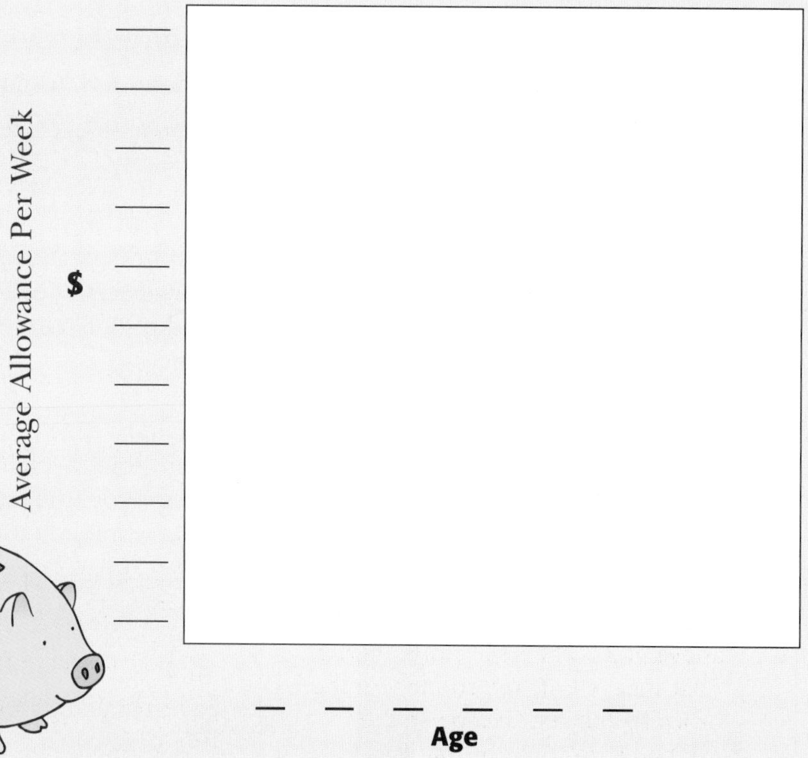

Average Allowance Per Week

$

Age

Source: www.kidsmoney.org

Text Feature

Graphs

Many textbooks, magazines, and newspapers contain graphs to illustrate information in the text. A **graph** is a diagram that shows numerical information in a visual way. A graph helps you "picture" the information and makes it easy to understand. You can also make comparisons at a glance and draw conclusions.

Step 1 **Read the title to find out what the graph is about.** The bar graph below compares animal and human hearing.

Step 2 **Read the labels to find out what is being compared.** The labels on the left side of the graph show the animals whose hearing is being measured. The labels at the bottom of the graph show sound frequencies in hertz.

Step 3 **Compare and contrast the information shown on the graph.** The bars of the graph show the frequency range for humans and each other animal listed. Compare the length of the bars. For example, can cats hear sounds at a higher frequency than dogs can?

Practice Your Skills!

1. Circle the label that tells which animal has the smallest frequency range.

2. Put an **X** on the name of the animal whose hearing is most similar to a dog's.

3. Underline the name of the animal with a frequency range from 1,000–120,000 Hz.

PAIR SHARE How would you compare the frequency range of humans and dolphins?

DID YOU HEAR THAT?

Sound is created by **vibrations** in the air. **Frequency** is the number of times an object vibrates per second. A sound's frequency determines how high or low the sound is. The higher the frequency, the higher the sound. The lower the frequency, the lower the sound. Scientists measure a sound's frequency in units called **hertz** (hurts), abbreviated Hz. The graph compares the frequencies of sounds heard by human beings and other animals.

Human ears hear sounds that have a frequency from 20 hertz to about 20,000 hertz. Sounds that are above 20,000 hertz are **ultrasonic**. That means they are too high to be heard by humans. However, they can be heard by some animals.

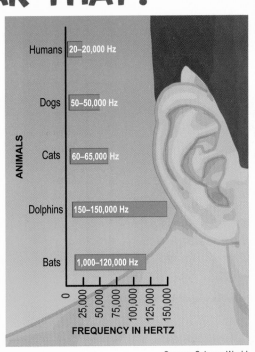

Animal	Frequency
Humans	20–20,000 Hz
Dogs	50–50,000 Hz
Cats	60–65,000 Hz
Dolphins	150–150,000 Hz
Bats	1,000–120,000 Hz

ANIMALS

FREQUENCY IN HERTZ

0 25,000 50,000 75,000 100,000 125,000 150,000

Source: Science World

Before You Read

Preview the article. Check (✔) the special features it has.

_____ title
_____ photos
_____ headings
_____ pronunciations
_____ graph
_____ boldfaced words

As You Read

- Did you read the title of the graph?
  ❏ Yes ❏ No

- Did you look at the labels?
  ❏ Yes ❏ No

- Did you compare the life spans of the various animals?
  ❏ Yes ❏ No

- Explain how you read the graph.

After You Read

1. Which facts show that many people treat their pets like their children?

2. If you wanted a long-living pet, which one would you choose?

PAIR SHARE Would you agree that each day is an adventure at Angell Memorial Animal Hospital? Explain why.

Angels of the Animal ER

Each day is an adventure at Angell Animal Medical Center, one of the oldest and largest animal hospitals in the country. On a typical day, worried "parents" bring a parade of sick pets into the **emergency room** (ER).

Our furry, feathered, or scaly friends are treated for everything from minor scratches and rashes to major life-threatening problems like cancer or being hit by a car.

Vets fixed up this dachshund with a wheelchair after he had back surgery.

From Cuts to Cancer

"You really never know what's going to come through the doors," says Barbara Castleman of the Massachusetts Society for the Prevention of Cruelty to Animals (MSPCA). One day in the ER, a five-foot boa constrictor covered in mites slithers in its cage. Two cockatiels squawk on their swings next to an overweight bulldog, who gags as he struggles to breathe.

A Big Responsibility

Angell Animal Medical Center treats 125 animals a day, and gets 50,000 visits from its **patients** each year. The animals receive much the same care that people do: hip replacements, pacemakers for their hearts, or chemotherapy if they have cancer.

This kind of care can be expensive—Americans spend about $12 billion a year on medical care for their pets.

Of course, some surgeries probably would only happen in the animal world. Once, doctors at Angell operated on a St. Bernard named Rosie who had a real taste for her owners' laundry. Veterinarians found socks, a towel, and a T-shirt inside Rosie's stomach. Rosie survived—and now her owners keep their laundry room locked.

Owning a pet is a big **responsibility.** Castleman says, "People need to have the time and resources to care for an animal."

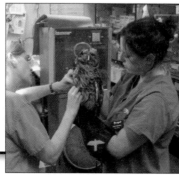

Angell staff assess an owl following a procedure.

Animals for the Ages

Animals are living longer and healthier lives these days because of big improvements in veterinary medicine. This graph shows the longest we can expect some of our favorite pets to live.

hamster

rabbit

iguana

dog

cat

parrot

0 10 20 30 40 50 60 70 80 90

Source: MSPCA

On Your Own

Read the article below. Then complete the circle graph to show the facts about reptile pets. Here's how:

- Give the graph a title.

- Find the largest section on the graph. Label it with the name of the most popular reptile pet. Also, write the percentage for that reptile.

- Continue in this way, matching the size of the sections with the percentages of reptile pets.

America's Pets

Scientists are finding that pets provide many benefits to people. They are good companions; they help to lower blood pressure during stressful situations, reduce loneliness, and can help older people feel more secure.

In 2003, Americans had more pets than ever before, with fish being the most popular pets. Next in popularity are cats. There were 77.7 million pet cats in our country! Dogs are the third most popular, with approximately 65 million living as pets. Birds follow in popularity. More than 17 million birds are kept as pets.

Scaly reptiles are slithering and leaping around in large numbers, as well. You may be surprised to find out that approximately 8.8 million reptiles live as pets in households in the United States! Of these reptiles, 40% are turtles, 23% are snakes, 19% are frogs or toads, and 18% are iguanas.

 Write two questions that can be answered by the graph. When you're done, exchange papers with a partner, and answer each other's questions.

1. _____

2. _____

Text Structure

Description

Before You Read

Vocabulary Fill in the chart to show how the words are related.

Words	How Are They Related?
tricycle tricolor	
ceremonial casual	
miniature giant	
replica model	

As You Read

Text Structure This article **describes** the White House, home of the president of the United States. To keep track of the details, underline words that describe how each room has been used. Circle the words that tell when certain events happened.

Text Feature How does the graph help you understand the article?

After You Read

1. In what ways was the 200th birthday of the White House celebrated?

2. Study the graph. How does the number of bedrooms compare with the number of bathrooms?

3. Choose a room in the White House. Describe its important characteristics and the events that took place in that room.

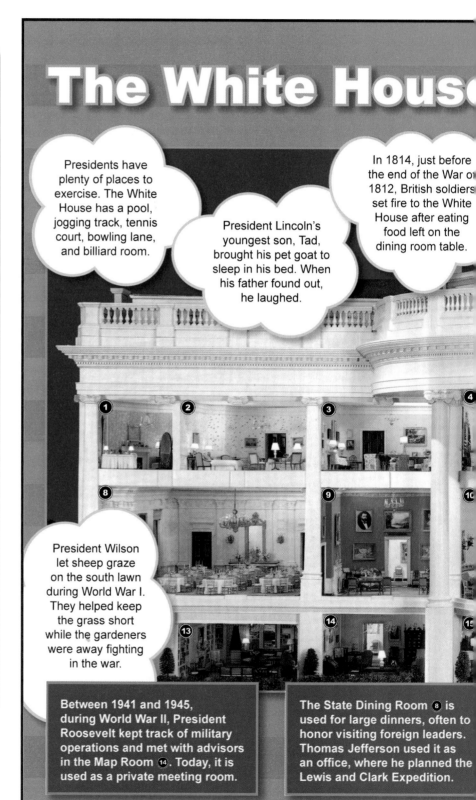

The White House

Presidents have plenty of places to exercise. The White House has a pool, jogging track, tennis court, bowling lane, and billiard room.

President Lincoln's youngest son, Tad, brought his pet goat to sleep in his bed. When his father found out, he laughed.

In 1814, just before the end of the War of 1812, British soldiers set fire to the White House after eating food left on the dining room table.

President Wilson let sheep graze on the south lawn during World War I. They helped keep the grass short while the gardeners were away fighting in the war.

Between 1941 and 1945, during World War II, President Roosevelt kept track of military operations and met with advisors in the Map Room ⑭. Today, it is used as a private meeting room.

The State Dining Room ⑧ is used for large dinners, often to honor visiting foreign leaders. Thomas Jefferson used it as an office, where he planned the Lewis and Clark Expedition.

Turned 200!

On November 1, 2000, the United States celebrated the birthday of its most important house—the White House.

The White House is the home of the president and the president's family. The White House also serves as an office where important laws are signed, a ceremonial (SER-uh-MOH-nee-uhl) setting for heads of state, and a museum that attracts more than 1 million visitors a year.

To mark its 200th birthday, special exhibits and ceremonies celebrated the White House's rich history. One display was of a miniature dollhouse of the White House (shown below), it was created by artists John and Jan Zweifel.

On November 1,1800, John Adams became the first president to move into the White House.

In the Lincoln Bedroom, in 1863, President Lincoln signed the Emancipation Proclamation.

The list below identifies the rooms in the White House Replica.

1. First Lady's Dressing Room
2. President's Bedroom
3. Family Sitting Room
4. Yellow Oval Room
5. Treaty Room
6. Lincoln Bedroom
7. Lincoln Sitting Room
8. State Dining Room
9. Red Room
10. Blue Room
11. Green Room
12. East Room
13. Library
14. Map Room
15. Diplomatic Reception Room
16. China Room
17. Vermeil Room

What's Inside the White House?

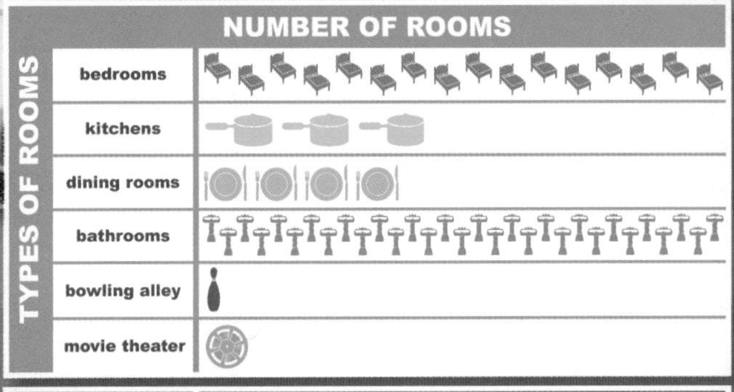

The East Room 12, the largest room in the White House, has been used for weddings, concerts, and bill signings. Since it has less furniture than any other room, it was a good place for President James Garfield's sons to ride around on tricycles while having a pillow fight.

TYPES OF ROOMS	NUMBER OF ROOMS	
bedrooms	🛏️🛏️🛏️🛏️🛏️🛏️🛏️🛏️🛏️🛏️🛏️🛏️🛏️🛏️	
kitchens	🍲🍲🍲	
dining rooms	🍽️🍽️🍽️🍽️	
bathrooms	🚰🚰🚰🚰🚰🚰🚰🚰🚰🚰🚰🚰🚰🚰🚰🚰🚰🚰🚰🚰🚰🚰🚰🚰🚰🚰	
bowling alley	🎳	
movie theater	🎞️	
KEY	**Each symbol stands for one room.**	

Description

Reread "The White House Turned 200!" Fill in the graphic organizer with details that describe each of the rooms.

The East Room

1. _____
2. _____
3. _____

State Dining Room

1. _____
2. _____
3. _____

Map Room

1. _____
2. _____
3. _____

Other Rooms

1. _____
2. _____
3. _____

 Use the graphic organizer above to retell "The White House Turned 200!" in your own words. Include as much information as you can remember.

Writing Frame

Use the information in your graphic organizer to fill in the writing frame.

The White House has many interesting features. It has a room called the

_____, which is _____.

It is used for _____.

The White House also has the _____.

Thomas Jefferson used it _____

_____.

Today, this room is used for _____.

Another room in the White House is the _____.

In this room, President Franklin Roosevelt _____

_____.

Today, this room is used as _____.

The White House also has _____

_____

_____.

 Use the writing frame above as a model to describe another well-known building, such as Mount Vernon, or a well-known structure, such as the Lincoln Memorial. Look in your social studies textbook if you need facts that will help you fill in the frame.

Text Feature

Primary Sources

Where would you go for an eyewitness account of something that happened in the past? You would look for a primary source. A **primary source** is an account of an event by a person who was there.

Primary sources may be oral, as in oral histories, or they may be written, such as newspaper articles and letters. They may be photos, and even artifacts—actual objects that have survived over time.

Step 1 **Read the title of the article to find out the topic.**

Step 2 **Preview the text.** Look for any primary source material. In the article, artifacts found on the ocean floor and parts of letters give first-hand information about a Civil War battleship.

Step 3 **Read the main article.** Sometimes the primary source material is in the article. Other times, it may be in a sidebar. If so, read this material after you read the main article.

Step 4 **Study the primary source material.** Pay attention to the time it is from. Ask yourself how the information adds to what you already know about the topic.

Practice Your Skills!

1. Put an **X** on the word that means "an object or tool from an earlier time."

2. Circle the year in which the *Monitor* sank.

3. What facts do the letter excerpts reveal that might not have been known before?

PAIR SHARE Why do you think historians are so interested in the artifacts that have been found?

Civil War Treasure Is Shipshape

After 140 years at the bottom of the sea, the last major piece of a Civil War battleship was recently recovered.

The gun turret, a structure that holds guns and moves in a circular direction, was the first of its kind and changed naval warfare.

As the world's first revolving gun turret, it is the most important artifact from the Civil War battleship USS *Monitor*. The turret was on the ocean floor since the *Monitor* sank during a storm off the coast of Cape Hatteras, North Carolina, in 1862.

SEA RELIC The turret is being raised.

Artifacts, such as this lantern, were recovered from the turret of the *Monitor*. Other recovered artifacts included 24 pieces of silver tableware with either the initials or names of crewmembers or officers aboard the *Monitor*.

The letters of *Monitor* crewman George Geer offer a rare view of a sailor's experience during the Civil War.

MARCH 2, 1862
I generally take the evenings to do my writing. Whenever I write, day or night in my stateroom, I have to use a candle, it is so dark...

MARCH 4, 1862
On Mondays, Wednesdays, and Saturdays we have Been soupe, or perhaps a better name would be to call it Been Water. I am often tempted to strip off my shirt and make a dive and see if there really is Beens in the Bottom...

Source: The Mariners' Museum, Newport News, Virginia

Practice Your Skills!

Before You Read

Preview the article. Check (✔) the special features it has.

_____ title
_____ photos
_____ graph
_____ captions
_____ primary sources
_____ map

As You Read

• Did you read the title and introduction?
❑ Yes ❑ No

• Did you look for primary sources?
❑ Yes ❑ No

• Explain how you read the article.

After You Read

1. How would you describe Melba as a person? Support your answer with examples from her interview.

2. Why were Melba's actions important to civil rights?

PAIR SHARE How did Melba's own words help you understand what happened? What did you learn from the photos?

The year is 1954. Melba Pattillo is 12 years old, smart, and black. She has good teachers in her all-black school in Little Rock, Arkansas. But her school is freezing in winter. Her books are old and worn. Schools for black children are supposed to be "equal" to those of white children. But they're not.

On May 17, 1954, the United States Supreme Court rules that separate public schools are illegal. The justices say that communities like Little Rock must let black children go to school with white children.

Melba volunteers to go to the all-white Central High School. Two years later, in September 1957, Melba and eight other African American students are enrolled at Central High. Melba is now 15 years old. Her life is about to change forever.

Here is Melba's story, in her own words, as she answered questions from students in an interview 40 years later.

Question: Why did you decide to go to Central?
Answer: We went to Central for opportunity . . . It was considered at the time one of America's finest schools. And that's what I wanted. My previous school got Central's old, used, greasy stuff. If something was broken and damaged it came to our school. My grandmother had this saying: "If you are not in the kitchen when they're slicing the pie, you will not get a share of it." . . .

Melba was 15 when she entered Central High School.

[We wanted] access to the pie; getting a slice of the American dream. We risked our lives for that.

Q: What was it like to go to school at Central?
A: The people who surrounded Central High School carried ropes to hang us with, guns and knives to kill us with . . . It was an angry, raging mob. And it was absolutely terrifying to walk past them. Every moment I wondered what would become of me. It was the kind of fear I had never known. And it went on most of the year.

Q: How did you keep your cool?
A: It wasn't easy to not fight back or talk back . . . I was so angry sometimes. Hot tears would come down my cheeks. And yet, even Martin Luther King told us: "Don't be selfish. Remember, you're doing this for future generations."

Q: What was it like meeting Martin Luther King, Jr?
A: Meeting Martin Luther King was a trip . . . I felt calmness, peace, and love. And I felt like "Oh, boy, I can be better than I am." . . . It was incredible.

On September 25, 1957, with soldiers all around her, Melba walks through the doors of Central High School. A soldier will walk her from class to class.

LITTLE ROCK

On Your Own

Some primary sources are inscriptions left behind by people who were passing through. Read each one and think about what it tells you.

Between 1910 and 1940, as many as 175,000 Chinese immigrants were detained in wooden barracks at Angel Island in San Francisco Bay for weeks, months, and even years. They left behind, carved on the wooden walls, a record of their experience.

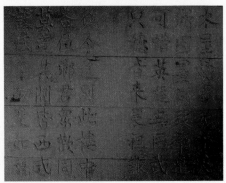

There are tens of thousands of poems composed on these walls.
They are all cries of complaint and sadness.
The day I am rid of this prison and attain success,
I must remember that this chapter once existed.

—By "One from Xiangshan" (Poem 31)

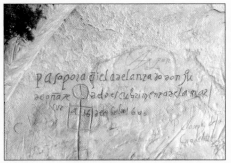

El Morro National Monument in New Mexico is sometimes called Inscription Rock. The huge sandstone landmark, with a waterhole at its base, became a popular stopping point for travelers. Many carved their signatures, dates, and messages before moving on.

Pioneers on the Oregon Trail carved their names to record their journey.

Use the primary source material above to complete the chart.

What is the primary source?	When was it made?	What does it tell you about the person and event?	What does it tell you about the time period?

Text Feature

Primary Sources

A **primary source** is an account of an event by someone who witnessed it.

Primary sources not only give you first-hand details of an event but also reveal the thoughts, feelings, and values of the people who were there at the time.

Step 1 **Read the title to find out what the article is about.**

Step 2 **Read the main article.** Sometimes the primary source material is in the article.

Step 3 **Study the primary source material.** Ask yourself, "How does this information add to what I know about the topic?"

Practice Your Skills!

1. Underline Carver's achievements.

2. Circle the word that tells what Carver believed measured success.

3. Put a check (✔) next to each type of primary source material.

PAIR SHARE What did you learn about George Washington Carver from his quotations?

George Washington Carver

George Washington Carver

George Washington Carver was born about 1864 (the exact year is unknown) on the Moses Carver farm in Diamond Grove, Missouri. His parents were slaves. As a boy, he liked to work in the garden, and he became very interested in plants.

After the Civil War, when George was 10 years old, he left the farm and went to Kansas. He was determined to get an education. He worked at various jobs to support himself as he attended school. In 1891, Carver became the first African American to enroll at the college which today is Iowa State University. He completed his master's degree and went to teach at Alabama's Tuskegee Institute. Carver worked there for the rest of his life, looking for ways to help people.

Carver developed a system of crop rotation, which he believed would keep the soil rich and improve the harvest. But he is best known for his knowledge of plant chemistry. His research resulted in the creation of 325 products from peanuts, more than 100 products from sweet potatoes, and hundreds more from other plants of the South.

A stamp honoring George Washington Carver.

George Washington Carver went from slavery to become a famous educator, scientist, and humanitarian. He died at Tuskegee on January 5, 1943.

These words of wisdom give us first-hand knowledge of the opinions of Carver.

"It is not the style of clothes one wears, neither the kind of automobile one drives, nor the amount of money one has in the bank, that counts. These mean nothing. It is simply service that measures success."
—G. W. Carver

"Ninety-nine percent of the failures come from people who have the habit of making excuses."
—G. W. Carver

BLIZZARD WARNING!

A tunnel dug through the snow in Farmington, Connecticut, after the blizzard of 1888.

Snow Plus Wind

Although many people use the term *blizzard* to describe any weather with a lot of snow, blizzards are really a special type of storm. In a true **blizzard**, the combination of falling and/or blowing snow plus sustained winds or frequent gusts of at least 35 miles an hour must lower the visibility to 1/4 mile or less for at least three hours in a row. Temperatures well below 32 degrees are typically associated with blizzards, too.

Snow Blowers

Strangely enough, blizzard conditions can occur without any snow actually falling from the sky. Strong winds can blow previously dumped snow, reducing the visibility to create blizzard conditions. Antarctica, which has some of the worst blizzards in the world, actually only gets a few inches of snow each year. But incredibly (in-KRED-uh-blee) cold temperatures mean the snow never melts. So when the wind blows, it's stirring up years' worth of old snow.

In the winter of 1888, a 15-year-old boy, O.W. Meier, and his two younger brothers battled a blizzard in Lincoln, Nebraska. Many years later, Mr. Meier still remembered that storm.

Beautiful big white flakes were falling fast the morning of that fateful day. At the last recess, the snow was about two feet deep. As swiftly as lightning, the storm struck the north side of the schoolhouse. The whole building shivered and quaked.

In an instant the room became black as night. The teacher said, "Those who live south may put on their coats and go, but the rest of you must stay here in this house."

We had not gone 16 feet when we found ourselves in a heavy drift of snow. We took hold of each other's hands and pulled ourselves out. The cold north wind blew us a half mile south. My brothers and I could not walk through the deep snow on the road, so we walked down the rows of corn stalks to keep from losing ourselves till we reached our pasture fence . . . .

For nearly a mile we followed the fence till we reached the corral and pens. The roaring wind and stifling snow blinded us so that we had to feel through the yard to the door of our house. Pa was shaking the ice and snow from his coat and boots. He had gone out to meet us but was forced back by the storm.

That was an awful night on the open plains. Many teachers and schoolchildren lost their lives in that blinding storm while trying to find their way home. The blizzard of 1888 has not been forgotten.

—From *American Life Histories: Manuscripts from the Federal Writers' Project*, 1936–1940

On Your Own

Use the information in this article to create a diary entry you might have written after experiencing the blizzard of 1888 in New York City. Include details that help the reader picture what the city looked like, what happened to you and people you knew, and how you felt about it.

The blizzard of 1888 affected New York City, as well as places farther west. In the city, the storm had 60 mph winds that created 50-foot-high snowdrifts. The temperature was below zero.

The snow was powder fine and fell so quickly that a footprint was covered in five minutes. When it was all over, there was 40 inches of snow on the ground in New York City.

Roads and highways were blocked. It was impossible to walk or even ride a horse. High winds whipped the fallen snow and caused debris to swirl in the air. Swinging signs crashed down on the street. There was no way to communicate, with telegraph and telephone wires and poles lying in tangles in the streets.

The snow caused a transportation crisis. Many people were stranded inside train cars that ran on elevated tracks. On one train, in order to reach the street, passengers climbed down a ladder that someone had put up to rescue them.

Hotels and even train stations were filled to capacity with stranded people. All schools were closed and no mail was delivered. At night, all the streets were dark.

Men quickly saw a chance to make money and hired out their snow-shoveling services. Newspapers reported that anyone could get as much as a dollar for clearing a sidewalk—not bad for 1888.

_____, 1888

We were just hit by an incredible blizzard!

_____

_____

_____

_____

_____

_____

_____

_____

_____

_____

_____

_____

_____

_____

_____

_____

_____

_____

Cause/Effect

Before You Read

Vocabulary Read the words from the article. Then fill in the chart. Put an **X** in the box to show whether the second word is a synonym, a related word, or an example of the first word.

What's the Connection?

Example	Synonym	Related Word
oceanographer oceanography		
corrode wear away		
submersibles submarines		
artifacts old coins		

As You Read

Text Structure This article tells about scientists who are reexamining the *Titanic* 20 years after it was first studied. As you read, underline the **causes** of changes to the ship. Circle the **effects**.

Text Feature How do the primary sources help you understand the article?

After You Read

1. Which facts show that the scientists were careful not to cause further damage to the ship?

2. Do you agree that it's important to document everything scientists find out about the *Titanic* as soon as possible. Why or why not?

ATTACK on the Titanic

Scientists returned to the famous ship they discovered almost 20 years ago. What they found may shock you.

Robert Ballard

On the cold, dark night of April 14, 1912, more than 2,000 people sailed across the Atlantic on a giant cruise ship called the R.M.S. *Titanic*. With hardly any warning, the ship scraped a massive **iceberg**. As water rushed into the ship, passengers scrambled to board lifeboats. When the ship sank three hours later, more than 1,500 people died.

The world's most famous shipwreck lay undisturbed until 1985. That year, **oceanographer** (OH-shun-OG-ruh-fer) Robert Ballard and his crew discovered the *Titanic*'s resting place deep in the North Atlantic. Harsh ocean conditions have caused the ship to **corrode** (kuh-RODE), and the crew suspected the damage would get worse over time.

Exactly how much has the ship corroded since its discovery? And why? In June 2004, Ballard led a team of scientists back to the *Titanic* to find out.

Dangers of the Deep

Titanic lies in the abyssal (uh-BISS-uhl) zone, a part of the ocean about 2.5 miles below the surface. Because the conditions in this zone are so harsh, few creatures live here. No light makes it to the sea floor, and temperatures hover around a chilly 35 degrees Fahrenheit.

The conditions in this zone also make it tough for a shipwreck. According to Dwight Coleman, a scientist and member of Ballard's crew, because the pressure of the water here is so strong, it's pushing *Titanic* into the ocean floor. "It's like there's an elephant standing on every square inch," he said.

The high levels of salt in the ocean also play a role in the ship's breakdown. Much of the *Titanic* is made from iron. When iron is placed in water, it will corrode over time. However, when salt is present in the water, that results in the metal corroding a lot faster.

Human visitors cause damage too. Markings show that **submersibles** have landed on the ship's deck, causing it to break.

And more that 6,000 artifacts, like coins and silverware, have been removed.

The *Titanic*'s Future

So, how long until the *Titanic* completely disappears? No one knows for sure, but many researchers believe that the famous shipwreck could be around for several more decades. Keeping visitors from disturbing the wreck may keep the ship intact much longer.

Therefore, scientists hope to document everything they can about the ship before it's destroyed. "It's like a museum down there, and it's not going to be there forever," said Coleman.

The Sinking of the *Titanic*

This is an eyewitness account from 8-year-old Marshall Drew, who was traveling with his aunt and uncle.

"When the *Titanic* struck the iceberg, I was in bed. However, for whatever reason I was awake and remember the jolt and cessation of motion. A steward knocked on the stateroom door and directed us to get dressed, put on life preservers and go to the boat deck, which we did… All was calm and orderly. An officer was in charge. 'Women and children first,' he said, as he directed lifeboat number 11 to be filled. There were many tearful farewells. We and Uncle Jim said good-bye… The lowering of the lifeboat 70 feet to the sea was perilous… Nothing worked properly, so that first one end of the lifeboat was tilted up and then far down.

I think it was the only time I was scared. Lifeboats pulled some distance away from the sinking *Titanic*, afraid of what suction might do… As row by row of the porthole lights of the *Titanic* sank into the sea this was about all one could see. When the *Titanic* upended to sink, all was blacked out until the tons of machinery crashed to the bow… As this happened hundreds and hundreds of people were thrown into the sea. It isn't likely I shall ever forget the screams of these people as they perished in water said to be 28 degrees… At this point in my life I was being brought up as a typical British kid. You were not allowed to cry. You were a 'little man.' So as a cool kid I lay down in the bottom of the lifeboat and went to sleep. When I awoke it was broad daylight…

JOURNEY TO THE *TITANIC*

To reach the shipwreck, robots traveled through three zones of the ocean: The photic (FOH-tik), the bathyal (BATH-ee-uhl), and the abyssal. The shipwreck was about 2.5 miles below the sea surface. That's 10 times the height of the Empire State Building.

Sea Surface

PHOTIC ZONE

200 meters (656 feet)

Robot Explorer

BATHYAL ZONE

Empire State Building

2,000 meters (6,562 feet)

ABYSSAL ZONE

Titanic wreckage

GREENLAND
ICELAND
CANADA
IRELAND
ENGLAND
Southampton
NEWFOUNDLAND
U.S.
New York
FRANCE
Location where the *Titanic* sank
Atlantic Ocean

The *Titanic* was supposed to sail from Southampton, England, to New York City.

The *Titanic*, shown here, sank during its first voyage.

"Rusticles" cover the ship's bow, or front.

Cause/Effect

Reread "Attack on the *Titanic*." Complete the graphic organizer to show the causes and effects of the shipwreck's breakdown.

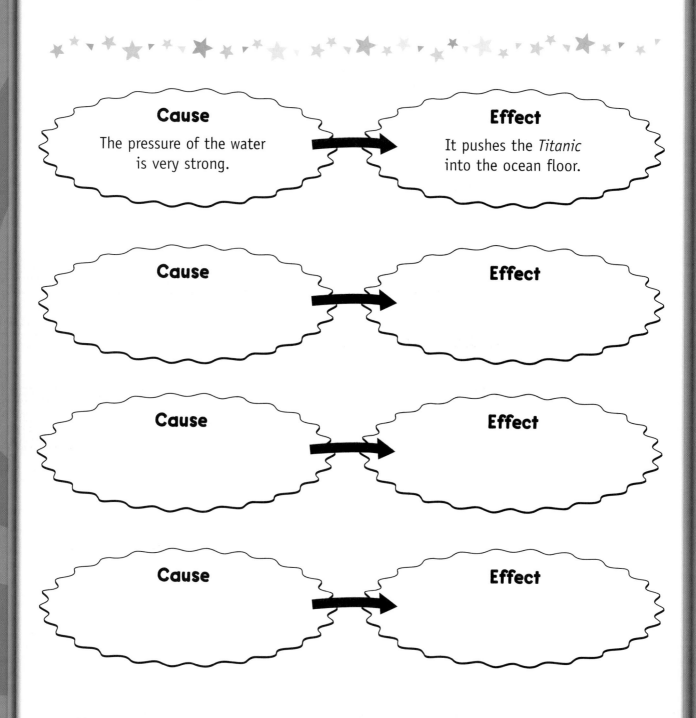

Cause
The pressure of the water is very strong.

Effect
It pushes the *Titanic* into the ocean floor.

Cause

Effect

Cause

Effect

Cause

Effect

Use the graphic organizer above to retell "Attack on the *Titanic*" in your own words. Include as much information as you can remember.

Writing Frame

Use the information in your graphic organizer to fill in the writing frame.

There are several causes for the *Titanic's* breakdown. One is the strong

water pressure in the ocean. The effect of this is that _____

_____.

Another reason for the breakdown is _____

_____. This explains why _____.

In addition, humans have caused damage to the shipwreck. Because

submersibles have landed on the *Titanic,* _____.

Other damage is due to _____.

They have _____.

For all these reasons, it is important that scientists _____

_____ as quickly as possible.

Use the writing frame above as a model to write about what caused
Christopher Columbus to set off from Spain and the effect of his landing
in America. Look in your social studies textbook if you need facts that
will help you fill in the frame.

Maps

A **map** is a flat picture of Earth. Maps can give you a lot of information in a limited space by using symbols and labels.

Step 1 **Read the map title.** It tells you what the map is about. The map below highlights the continent of Asia.

Step 2 **Find any map symbols.** A symbol stands for a real thing or place. It may be a picture or a special color. A **map key** or **legend** tells what each map symbol means. A **scale** shows the relationship between distances shown on the map and real distances.

Step 3 **Read the labels.** These are important words to remember. Each label tells the name of a geographic location.

Step 4 **Look at the locator map.** The locator map is a small map placed inside the larger map. It shows where Asia is located in relation to other continents in the world.

Practice Your Skills!

1. Put an **X** on the name of the country in which Yao Ming is a citizen.

2. Circle the name of the body of water to the east of Japan.

3. Which country borders Mongolia to the north?

PAIR SHARE What information would you use to convince someone that Asia is a continent with varied climates, cultures, and governments?

Standing TALL

Asians make up 4.2 percent of the U.S. population. They represent more than 20 countries, including China, India, Vietnam, and South Korea (see map). Asians are the nation's smallest minority group—but they are growing quickly. Between 1990 and 2000, the number of Asians in the U.S. grew 48 percent, according to the U.S. Census Bureau.

Asians' influence on the U.S. is vast. They are making their mark in fields as varied as sports, government, and entertainment.

Basketball Star

When Houston Rockets center Yao Ming, of China, hits the court, it's not only his 7-foot, 5-inch height that is impressive. It is the skill with which Yao handles the basketball. He has not only won the admiration of sports fans, he has also won the hearts of many Asian Americans.

Teen Golfer

Six-foot-tall Michelle Wie is a Korean-American born in Hawaii. Still in her teens, she is already head and shoulders above the competition in professional golf.

Yao's and Michelle's athletic accomplishments add another dimension to the influence of Asians on U.S. society.

ASIA

ARCTIC OCEAN

RUSSIA

KAZAKHSTAN

MONGOLIA

AZERBAIJAN
GEORGIA UZBEKISTAN
ARMENIA KYRGYZSTAN
TURKEY TURKMENISTAN
CYPRUS SYRIA TAJIKISTAN
LEBANON IRAQ IRAN AFGHANISTAN
ISRAEL JORDAN
KUWAIT PAKISTAN
BAHRAIN
QATAR U.A.E.
SAUDI
ARABIA OMAN
YEMEN

NORTH KOREA JAPAN
SOUTH KOREA

CHINA

NEPAL BHUTAN

BANGLADESH

MYANMAR (BURMA)

INDIA LAOS

THAILAND

VIETNAM

CAMBODIA

SRI LANKA

MALDIVES

BRUNEI
MALAYSIA

SINGAPORE

TAIWAN

PACIFIC OCEAN

PHILIPPINES

N
W E
S

INDIAN OCEAN

INDONESIA

Practice Your Skills!

Before You Read

Preview the article. Check (✔) the special features it has.

_____ headings
_____ graph
_____ map
_____ compass rose
_____ photo
_____ boldfaced words

As You Read

- Did you read the title of the map?
  ❏ Yes ❏ No

- Did you read each map label?
  ❏ Yes ❏ No

- Did you read the map key to find out what each color stands for?
  ❏ Yes ❏ No

- Explain how you read the map.

After You Read

1. Where is French spoken in Latin America?

2. What language is spoken in the greatest number of countries in Latin America?

PAIR SHARE What do the languages spoken in each country tell you about that country's history?

A New WORLD

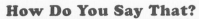

Kids of Hispanic immigrants rise to the challenge of adjusting to life in the United States

Jair (pronounced JAH-ear) Saenz, 10, is at home on the soccer field. He is at home playing with his friends. He is at home in his new hometown of Akron, Pennsylvania.

Three years ago, Jair didn't know Akron, or the people in it. He didn't even know the language they spoke.

Jair is one of millions of immigrants from Latin America (see map) who have come to the United States in recent years. According to the U.S. Census, more than 1.8 million kids in America today came to the U.S. from Latin American countries. Jair and his family emigrated from Peru to the United States three years ago.

In total, Hispanics make up almost 13.5 percent of the U.S. population. That makes Latinos the largest—and most rapidly growing—minority group in the United States. Latino culture is a growing and rich part of American culture.

A New Land

Immigrating to another country can be difficult for many reasons.

There are often language and cultural barriers that make everyday events like shopping and attending school difficult. Then there's the challenge of making friends.

How Do You Say That?

For Jair, the key to fitting in was learning English. When he arrived in the United States, Jair couldn't understand what was being said on TV. He didn't understand what other neighborhood kids were saying. He didn't understand his teacher on his first day of school.

A Fluent Life

It was tough at first, he says, but little by little he learned English. Playing sports with neighborhood boys and in leagues also helped. At first, he would not say a word on the soccer field, but now he often shouts directions to his teammates during their games.

These days, Jair is free to concentrate—not so much on learning a new language, but on diving for soccer balls headed for the net.

Hispanics are people of Spanish-speaking descent, or ancestry. That means that their family line can be traced to countries where the dominant language is Spanish. Some Hispanic people in the United States come from Spain, but most Hispanic Americans, or their ancestors, hail from Mexico, Central and South America, and the Caribbean. Collectively, those places are known as Latin America—and that's why many Hispanics prefer to be called Latinos.

KEY

Latin America
- English-speaking
- Spanish-speaking
- French-speaking
- Portuguese-speaking
- Dutch-speaking
- Spanish/English-speaking

On Your Own

The map below shows where U.S. immigrants came from between 1870 and 1924. The graph shows the number of immigrants that came from which area. Think about how the information in the map and graph add to what you already know about immigration today.

🌐 Read the map title and labels and the graph title and labels.

🌐 Study the map and graph carefully.

🌐 Think about the information they show. For example, ask yourself, "Why may have some immigrants landed on a particular coast of the United States?"

Immigration to the U.S. Between 1870 and 1924

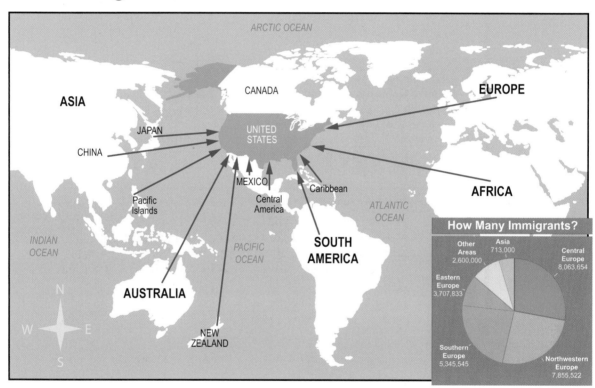

 Put a ✔ in front of each question that can be answered by the map and graph. Then, write other questions about the map and graph. When you're done, change papers with a partner. Answer each other's questions.

❏ 1. From which region did most immigrants come during this time period?

❏ 2. From which continents did immigrants land on the West Coast of the United States?

❏ 3. From which country did the most immigrants come?

    4. My own question_____

Text Feature

Maps

A **map** is a flat picture of Earth. Maps can give you a lot of information in a limited space by using symbols and labels.

Step 1 **Read the map title.** It tells you what the map is about.

Step 2 **Find the map symbols.** A symbol stands for a real thing or place. The **map key** or **legend** tells what each map symbol means. The map scale tells the relationship between distances on a map and real distances.

Step 3 **Read the labels.** These are important words to remember.

Step 4 **Look at the locator map.** The locator map is a small map set on the main map. It shows where the area of the main map is located in relation to other landforms.

Practice Your Skills!

1. Put an **X** on the name of the ocean at the North Pole.

2. Circle the name of the island closest to the Ward Hunt Ice Shelf.

3. Underline the names of the countries near the North Pole.

PAIR SHARE Do you think the rise in Earth's temperature will cause problems for people living in the United States? Why or why not?

ARCTIC REGION

A 3,000-year-old sheet of Arctic ice, so big it would cover roughly half of Rhode Island, has cracked in half, raising new concerns about global warming. Higher temperatures likely caused the Ward Hunt Ice Shelf, the largest ice shelf in the Arctic, to break in two. Researchers aren't sure that global warming, the gradual rise in Earth's temperature, is to blame. But they say that the breakup of the Ward Hunt fits a pattern of recent events that have been linked to the phenomenon.

One thing is certain: Earth's temperature is on the rise.

Melting ice is not good news for polar bears. The big, white beasts walk across the Arctic ice to get to their food supply—seals swimming in the ocean. Warmer temperatures melt the ice sooner, giving the polar bears less time to catch and eat seals.

Arctic

Arctic Circle

RUSSIA

FINLAND

SWEDEN
Oslo★
NORWAY

North Pole 90° N
+

Pacific Ocean

Arctic Ocean

ICELAND
★Reykjavik

Alaska
(U.S.)

GREENLAND
(Kalaallit nunaat)
(Denmark)

Nuuk★

Atlantic Ocean

★Juneau
CANADA

KEY

★ Country Capital
★ U.S. State Capital
● Area where Ward Hunt Ice Shelf broke apart

Practice Your Skills!

Before You Read

Preview the article. Check (✔) the special features it has.

_____ title
_____ headings
_____ labels
_____ pronunciations
_____ map
_____ boldfaced words

As You Read

- Did you read the title of the map?
  ❏ Yes ❏ No

- Did you read each map label?
  ❏ Yes ❏ No

- Did you study the photographs inset on the map?
  ❏ Yes ❏ No

- Explain what you learned by reading the map.

After You Read

1. What is a **biome**?

2. What are the characteristics of a tropical rain forest?

PAIR SHARE Discuss why scientists are worried about maintaining a balance in biomes.

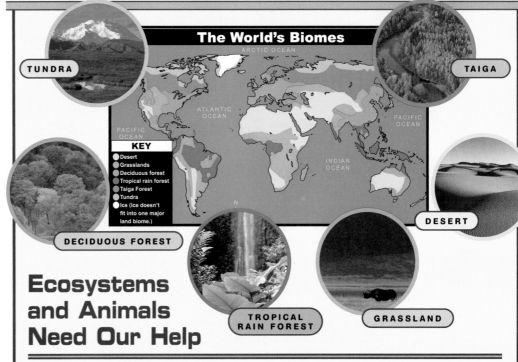

The World's Biomes

ARCTIC OCEAN

TUNDRA

TAIGA

ATLANTIC OCEAN

PACIFIC OCEAN

PACIFIC OCEAN

INDIAN OCEAN

KEY
- Desert
- Grasslands
- Deciduous forest
- Tropical rain forest
- Taiga Forest
- Tundra
- Ice (Ice doesn't fit into one major land biome.)

N

DESERT

DECIDUOUS FOREST

TROPICAL RAIN FOREST

GRASSLAND

Ecosystems and Animals Need Our Help

The land on Earth is divided into six major kinds of large ecosystems, called **biomes** (BIGH-ohmz). Each biome has its own climate, soil, plants, and animals. The animals and plants in these biomes survive because all parts of the biome work together.

Taiga, one biome, has very cold winters and cool summers. Plants consist mostly of spruce, fir, and other evergreen trees. Animals include rodents, snowshoe hares, lynx, sable, ermine, wolves, caribou, bears, and wolves. Birds appear only in summer.

Deciduous forests are a second biome. They have relatively mild summers and cold winters. A variety of hardwood trees grow here. Wolves, deer, bears, small mammals, birds, amphibians, reptiles, and insects inhabit this biome.

In **tropical rain forests**, the climate is hot all year and there is a great deal of rain. The largest variety of plants and animals call this biome their home.

Desert biomes are generally very hot during the day and cool at night. Few plants survive in this dry climate, and animal life consists of rodents, snakes, and some birds. Hot deserts, like those in Australia, stay toasty all year, while cold deserts, such as the Gobi desert, can be chilly.

Very cold, harsh, and long winters are typical of **tundra**. Summers are short and cool. Grasses, wildflowers, mosses, and small shrubs can survive in this biome. Most residents, such as migrating caribou, snowshoe hares, owls, and hawks use the tundra as a summer home. Some polar bears live in this climate year round.

Grasslands are cool in winter and hot in summer, with moderate rainfall. Grasses, small shrubs, and some trees thrive in this biome. A large variety of small animals live in American grasslands. African grasslands include larger animals, such as elephants, lions, zebras, and giraffes.

Humans can destroy the delicate balance in a biome. They do this by building too many houses, farming the land, and cutting down trees. As a result, animals and plants in biomes are losing their homes.

Many scientists, organizations, and governments are working to maintain the balance of nature in biomes. For example, to help endangered butterflies in the American grasslands, conservationists are planting lupine seeds to restore the plant whose nectar provides food for the Fender's blue butterfly.

On Your Own

Below is an article and map about the Amazon rain forest. Read the article.
Then complete the map. Remember to:

- Give the map a title.

- Complete the compass rose by writing N, E, W, and S in the correct place.

- Circle the frontier forests with medium or high threat of deforestation.

What's Happening to "The World's Lung"?

"Frontier forests" are areas that are relatively undisturbed by human activity and are large enough to maintain their **biodiversity** (BI-o-dih-VUR-sih-tee), including populations of many species of plants and animals. At one time, the Amazon rain forest contained, for the most part, frontier forests. Today, much of the area contains non-frontier forests. Non-frontier forests were formerly frontier forests but, over time, have been developed for large farms and housing.

The Amazon rain forest is sometimes called "the world's lung." Because it contains billions of trees, the rain forest absorbs more carbon dioxide than it releases. Carbon dioxide is a gas that traps the sun's heat close to Earth and contributes to global warming. The rain forest absorbs carbon dioxide that is produced by cars and factories around the world and that is just one of the reasons it is important to preserving our planet.

Logging, ranching, and development have destroyed almost a quarter of the Amazon. These activities are limiting the ability of the rain forest to absorb carbon dioxide and protect Earth's temperature from dangerous warming.

Scientists are concerned with the level of deforestation; the removal of the forest, as a result of human activities. The map shows the level of threat from logging, ranching, and development in different regions of the rain forest.

MAP TITLE _____

Caribbean Sea

Caracas

VENEZUELA

Georgetown
Paramaribo

GUYANA

SURINAME

Cayenne
FRENCH GUIANA
(Fr.)

ATLANTIC
OCEAN

Bogotá

COLOMBIA

Quito

ECUADOR

PERU

Lima

BRAZIL

La Paz

BOLIVIA

Sucre

Brasília

PACIFIC
OCEAN

PARAGUAY

Asunción

ATLANTIC
OCEAN

ARGENTINA

Santiago

CHILE

Buenos Aires

URUGUAY
Montevideo

San Matías Gulf

Gulf of San Jorge

Bahía
Grande

Strait of Magellan

South America

0   250   500   750 mi

0   250   500   750 1000 km

CAPTION

_____
_____
_____

KEY

- **Frontier forests:** Medium to high threat of deforestation
- **Frontier forests:** Low or no threat of deforestation
- **Frontier forests:** Not assessed for threat of deforestation
- **Non-frontier forests**

Text Structure

Problem/Solution

PRESERVING

Before You Read

Vocabulary Read the words pairs from the article. Think about how each pair of words go together. Fill in the chart with a sentence or phrase that explains the relationship.

What's the Connection?

Words	How They Go Together
ancestors heritage	
restore preserve	
tongue language	

As You Read

Text Structure This article presents the **problem** of saving Native American languages and the ways people are trying to **solve** this problem. To keep track of the problem, underline sentences that describe the problem. Circle the sentences that tell how people are trying to solve it.

Text Feature How does the map help you understand the article? What information does it add?

After You Read

1. Why do Native Americans want to learn to speak the language of their ancestors?

2. Study the map. Where is Eskimo-Aleut spoken?

3. What do you think are the best ways to help young people learn about their heritage? Why?

Members of the Mutsun and Miami Native American tribes are working hard to revive their native languages—a big part of their culture.

Major Native American Language Families in 2002

KEY
- Algonquian
- Caddoan
- Eskimo-Aleut
- Hokan
- Iroquoian
- Muskogean
- Na-dene
- Penutian
- Salishan
- Siouan
- Uto-Aztecan

How did the Dr. Seuss children's classic *Green Eggs and Ham* help to save a Native American language?

With the help of an expert, members of the Amah Mutsun (moot-SOON) tribe in California translated the Dr. Seuss classic into Mutsun—*tcutsu motRe yuu totRe*—in order to pass the language onto their children.

Quirina Luna-Costillas and her cousin, Lisa Carrier, led that effort. The two women—like many other Native Americans—are working to restore and preserve the language of their ancestors. Language is an important part of a people's history and culture.

Lost Languages

Mutsun is one of many Native American tongues that have been all but lost. About 300 Native American languages were spoken when Columbus landed in 1492. Today, only 175 of those languages are spoken, according to the **Indigenous** (in-DIJ-uh-ness) Language Institute in New Mexico.

The problem occurred for

How Do You Say It?

In English: "Hello, how are you?"

In Mutsun Language: misYmin tRuuhis hinkatem (mish-meen true-hees hinka-tem).

In Miami Language: Aya neehahki-nko kiiyawi (EYE-yah-NAY-hahg-kengo key-AH wi).

several reasons. First, when tribes were forced from their land by settlers, many of the speakers simply perished. Second, many others were sent to boarding schools and were forbidden to speak a language other than English.

As a result, today, few languages are spoken by enough young people to ensure that the languages will be passed on.

In an attempt to solve the problem, some tribes are videotaping elder members who speak the language. In other tribes, children are being taught language in intense programs, or by their parents.

New Generations Learn

Luna-Costillas started teaching Mutsun to her daughter four years ago. She and her team were able to piece together the Mutsun language by recalling personal memories of their ancestors. She also found a book by a Spanish missionary that listed hundreds of Mutsun words. They try to learn a new word each day.

Others Are Doing the Same

Daryl Baldwin is also working to protect his people's native language. Baldwin is a member of the Oklahoma Miami tribe in the Midwestern United States.

He directs the Myaamia (mee-ah-mee-ah) Project of Miami University in Oxford, Ohio. The Myaamia Project helps restore,

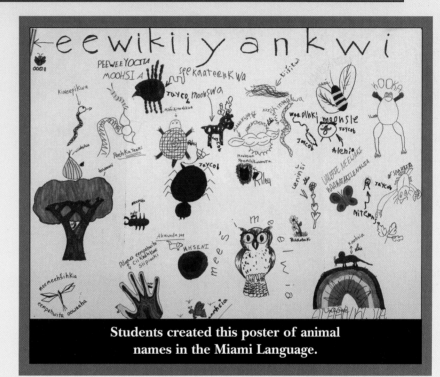

Students created this poster of animal names in the Miami Language.

preserve, and promote the Miami Nation's history, culture, and language. The language disappeared in the early 1960s.

"We wanted to bring our language back into everyday life," says Baldwin.

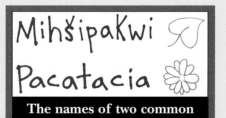

The names of two common objects in the Miami language.

A Family Tradition

Baldwin's father taught him his **heritage**. Through oral tradition, he learned of the ancestral names of his forefathers. Now his children are learning the same things.

"If we didn't keep the language alive," said Baldwin's son, Jarrid, who is 11, "we'd lose the language and the culture."

Problem/Solution

Reread "Preserving a Proud Past." Fill in the graphic organizer by identifying the main problem in the article, the attempted solutions, and the end result.

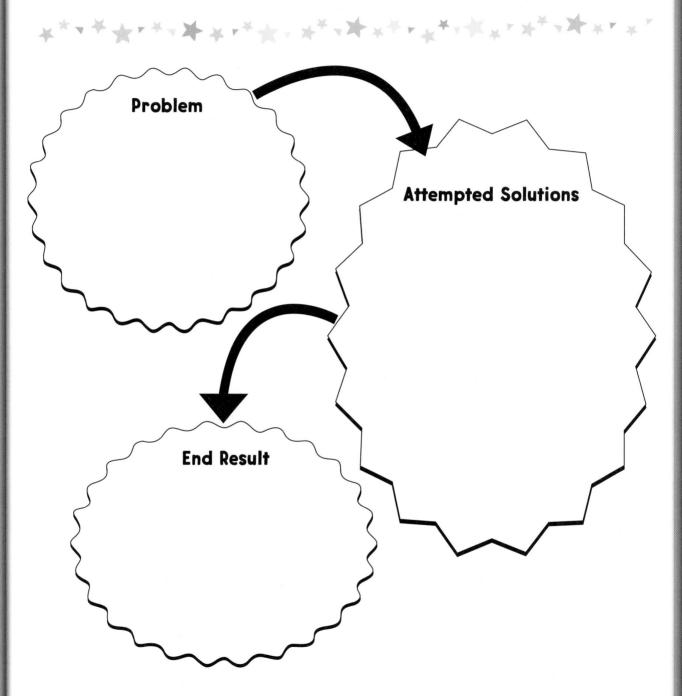

Problem

Attempted Solutions

End Result

Use the graphic organizer above to retell "Preserving a Proud Past" in your own words. Include as much information as you can remember.

Writing Frame

Use the information in your graphic organizer to fill in the writing frame.

Many Native Americans are working hard to preserve their past.

The problem is that _____

_____

_____.

The problem happened because _____

_____

_____.

The problem is being solved by _____

_____

_____

_____.

Now younger Native Americans are learning about their heritage and

helping to preserve the past.

Use the writing frame above as a model to write about how another group of people, such as another Native American tribe, has solved the problem of preserving its culture. Look in your social studies textbook if you need facts that will help you fill in the frame.

Text Feature

Time Lines

Some time lines have more than one tier. Each tier, or part of the time line, can show events that occurred at different places at the same time. It can also show different types of events that occurred in the same place. Multi-tiered time lines show the relationship between events and how events affect each other during a time period.

Step 1 **Read the title and instruction to find out the topic or historical period covered in the time line.**
The title of the time line below tells that it will be about our nation's capital, Washington, D.C.

Step 2 **Look at the titles of each tier.** They tell you the time period, part of the world, or subject area in which each event took place.

Step 3 **Find the starting and ending dates for the time line.**
Some time lines, such as this one, are vertical. You read them from top to bottom. Others are horizontal. You read them from left to right.

Step 4 **Read the labels for each date. They describe each event.**

Practice Your Skills!

1. Put an **X** on the date that shows when a president first lived in the White House.

2. Circle the label that names the structure built to honor the first president.

3. In what year was a museum dedicated to U.S. Native Americans opened?

PAIR SHARE How are the two time line tiers related?

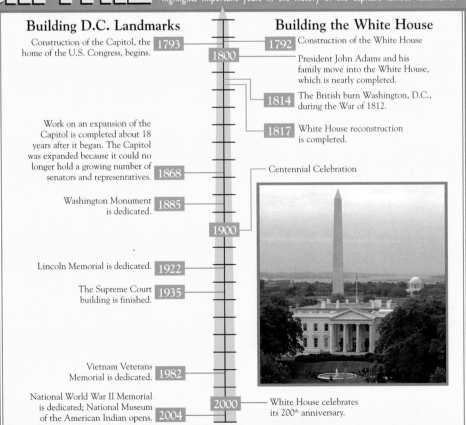

BUILDING THE CAPITAL

Construction of the White House began shortly after George Washington chose the site for the nation's capital. But it took decades for many of the most famous structures of Washington, D.C., to be designed and built. The time line highlights important years in the history of the capital's famous landmarks.

Building D.C. Landmarks

Construction of the Capitol, the home of the U.S. Congress, begins. **1793**

Work on an expansion of the Capitol is completed about 18 years after it began. The Capitol was expanded because it could no longer hold a growing number of senators and representatives. **1868**

Washington Monument is dedicated. **1885**

Lincoln Memorial is dedicated. **1922**

The Supreme Court building is finished. **1935**

Vietnam Veterans Memorial is dedicated. **1982**

National World War II Memorial is dedicated; National Museum of the American Indian opens. **2004**

Building the White House

1792 Construction of the White House

1793

1800

President John Adams and his family move into the White House, which is nearly completed.

1814 The British burn Washington, D.C., during the War of 1812.

1817 White House reconstruction is completed.

Centennial Celebration

1900

2000 White House celebrates its 200th anniversary.

Before You Read

Preview the article. Check (✔) the special features it has.

_____ title
_____ dates
_____ labels
_____ map
_____ flow chart

As You Read

- Did you read the title of the time line?
  ❏ Yes ❏ No

- Did you read the beginning and ending dates?
  ❏ Yes ❏ No

- Did you compare the events happening in different countries at the same time?
  ❏ Yes ❏ No

- Explain how you read the time line.

After You Read

1. In which countries did advances in transportation occur between 1800 and 1850?

2. Which sporting events are included on the time line? Where and when did they take place?

PAIR SHARE How many years passed between the start of the American Revolution and the beginning of the Mexican Revolution?

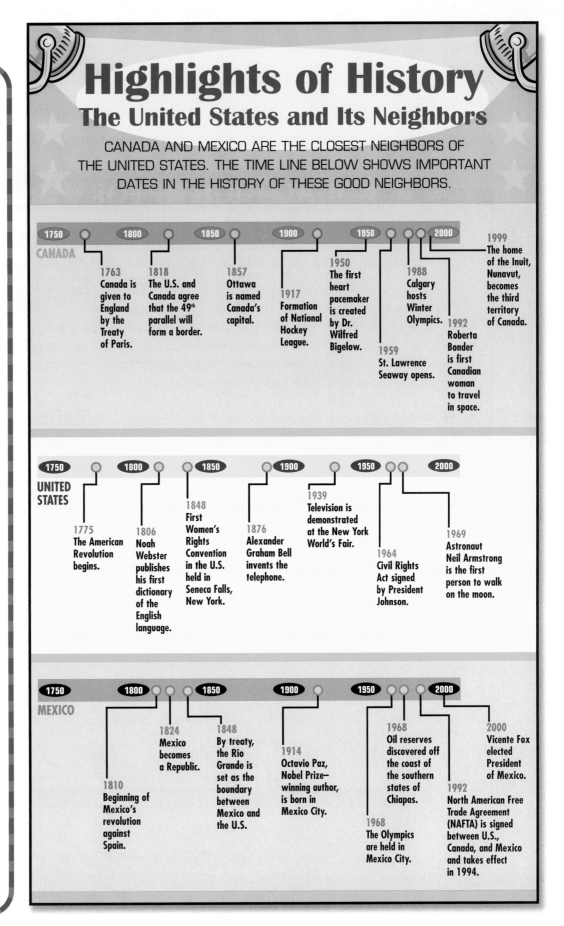

Highlights of History
The United States and Its Neighbors

CANADA AND MEXICO ARE THE CLOSEST NEIGHBORS OF THE UNITED STATES. THE TIME LINE BELOW SHOWS IMPORTANT DATES IN THE HISTORY OF THESE GOOD NEIGHBORS.

CANADA

1763 Canada is given to England by the Treaty of Paris.

1818 The U.S. and Canada agree that the 49th parallel will form a border.

1857 Ottawa is named Canada's capital.

1917 Formation of National Hockey League.

1950 The first heart pacemaker is created by Dr. Wilfred Bigelow.

1959 St. Lawrence Seaway opens.

1988 Calgary hosts Winter Olympics.

1992 Roberta Bonder is first Canadian woman to travel in space.

1999 The home of the Inuit, Nunavut, becomes the third territory of Canada.

UNITED STATES

1775 The American Revolution begins.

1806 Noah Webster publishes his first dictionary of the English language.

1848 First Women's Rights Convention in the U.S. held in Seneca Falls, New York.

1876 Alexander Graham Bell invents the telephone.

1939 Television is demonstrated at the New York World's Fair.

1964 Civil Rights Act signed by President Johnson.

1969 Astronaut Neil Armstrong is the first person to walk on the moon.

MEXICO

1810 Beginning of Mexico's revolution against Spain.

1824 Mexico becomes a Republic.

1848 By treaty, the Rio Grande is set as the boundary between Mexico and the U.S.

1914 Octavio Paz, Nobel Prize–winning author, is born in Mexico City.

1968 Oil reserves discovered off the coast of the southern states of Chiapas.

1968 The Olympics are held in Mexico City.

1992 North American Free Trade Agreement (NAFTA) is signed between U.S., Canada, and Mexico and takes effect in 1994.

2000 Vicente Fox elected President of Mexico.

On Your Own

Below is the first tier of a time line showing important dates in the Civil Rights Movement. Use the information in the article to create a second tier for the time line.

EQUAL RIGHTS FOR ALL

Between the early 1950s and the year 2000, African Americans, women, the elderly, and people with disabilities all fought for equal treatment under the law.

Women first won the right to vote in 1920. But they still did not have other rights that men had. During the 1960s, women's roles began to change. In 1966, The National Organization for Women was formed by Betty Friedan to help women win equal rights. Women started being elected to public office. An example is Shirley Chisolm, who in 1968 became the first African-American woman elected to the House of Representatives.

In 1923 Alice Paul had introduced the Equal Rights Amendment. It took until 1972 for the Senate and the House of Representatives to pass that legislation.

In 1981 Sandra Day O'Connor became the first woman appointed to the Supreme Court and in 1993 Ruth Bader Ginsburg also was named to that high court.

Older people and people with disabilities also fought for equality during these years. In 1972 Maggie Kuhn formed the Gray Panthers, an organization that helped to pass a law making it illegal to force workers over 65 to retire. The Americans With Disabilities Act, which was passed in 1990, made it illegal for employers to discriminate against people with disabilities.

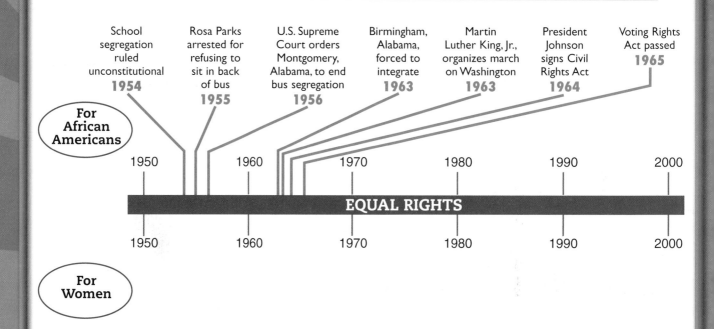

School segregation ruled unconstitutional **1954**

Rosa Parks arrested for refusing to sit in back of bus **1955**

U.S. Supreme Court orders Montgomery, Alabama, to end bus segregation **1956**

Birmingham, Alabama, forced to integrate **1963**

Martin Luther King, Jr., organizes march on Washington **1963**

President Johnson signs Civil Rights Act **1964**

Voting Rights Act passed **1965**

For African Americans

1950   1960   1970   1980   1990   2000

EQUAL RIGHTS

1950   1960   1970   1980   1990   2000

For Women

Text Feature

Time Lines

A **time line** can have more than one tier. Multi-tiered time lines show the relationship between events and how events affect each other during a time period.

Step 1 **Read the title and introduction to find out the topic and historical period covered in the time line.** The time line below shows events in the life of Benjamin Franklin and advances in science and technology that took place during the period in which he lived.

Step 2 **Look at the titles of each tier.** They tell you the time period, part of the world, or subject area in which each event took place.

Step 3 **Find the starting and ending dates for the time line.**

Step 4 **Read the labels for each date.** The labels give information about important dates and events in Franklin's life and the technical and scientific changes that were occurring during that time.

Practice Your Skills!

1. Put an **X** on the date that shows when Franklin proved that lightning is electricity.

2. (Circle) the events that happened during the 1750s.

3. Was the first patient vaccinated against smallpox before or after the invention of bifocal eyeglasses?

PAIR SHARE Which facts would you choose to show that Ben Franklin was interested in government as well as science?

Ben Franklin: His Place in History

Ben Franklin's natural curiosity about the way things work led to his many inventions. During his lifetime, many other inventors also improved people's lives through their creative ideas and devices.

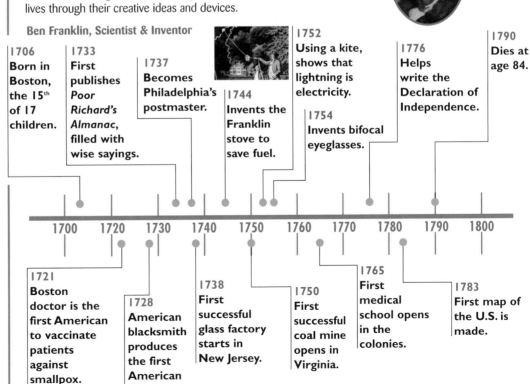

Ben Franklin, Scientist & Inventor

1706 Born in Boston, the 15th of 17 children.

1733 First publishes *Poor Richard's Almanac*, filled with wise sayings.

1737 Becomes Philadelphia's postmaster.

1744 Invents the Franklin stove to save fuel.

1752 Using a kite, shows that lightning is electricity.

1754 Invents bifocal eyeglasses.

1776 Helps write the Declaration of Independence.

1790 Dies at age 84.

1700 1720 1730 1740 1750 1760 1770 1780 1790 1800

1721 Boston doctor is the first American to vaccinate patients against smallpox.

1728 American blacksmith produces the first American steel.

1738 First successful glass factory starts in New Jersey.

1750 First successful coal mine opens in Virginia.

1765 First medical school opens in the colonies.

1783 First map of the U.S. is made.

Other Inventions & Advances

97

Practice Your Skills!

Before You Read

Preview the article. Check (✔) the special features it has.

_____ title
_____ pictures
_____ introduction
_____ captions
_____ map
_____ boldfaced words

As You Read

• Did you read the title of the time line?
❑ Yes ❑ No

• Did you read the introduction?
❑ Yes ❑ No

• Did you compare the dates and events on the time line?
❑ Yes ❑ No

• Explain how you read the time line.

After You Read

1. Which important inventions occurred during the 1870s?

2. Were the first practical electric lights invented before or after the telephone?

PAIR SHARE Which inventions show that Edison made important contributions to entertainment?

A Time for Inventions

Thomas Edison said, "I never perfected an invention that I did not think about in terms of the service it might give others . . . I find out what the world needs, then I proceed to invent . . . ." Indeed, he was one of the greatest and most productive inventors of his time. And he had lots of competition! He lived during a time when many other inventors were achieving technological firsts.

Thomas Edison

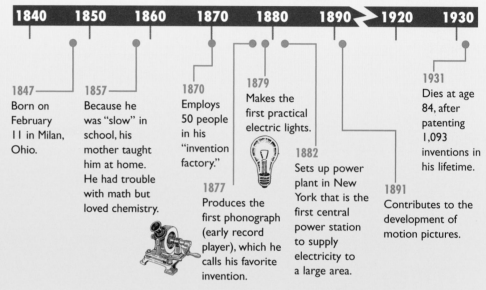

1840 1850 1860 1870 1880 1890 1920 1930

1847 — Born on February 11 in Milan, Ohio.

1857 — Because he was "slow" in school, his mother taught him at home. He had trouble with math but loved chemistry.

1870 Employs 50 people in his "invention factory."

1877 Produces the first phonograph (early record player), which he calls his favorite invention.

1879 Makes the first practical electric lights.

1882 Sets up power plant in New York that is the first central power station to supply electricity to a large area.

1891 Contributes to the development of motion pictures.

1931 Dies at age 84, after patenting 1,093 inventions in his lifetime.

Technology Firsts 1850–1930

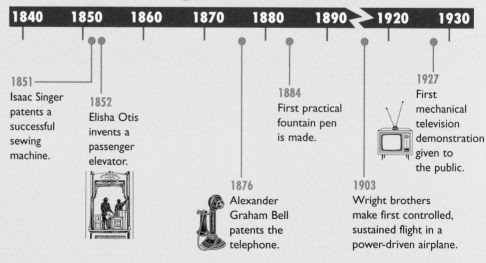

1840 1850 1860 1870 1880 1890 1920 1930

1851 — Isaac Singer patents a successful sewing machine.

1852 Elisha Otis invents a passenger elevator.

1876 Alexander Graham Bell patents the telephone.

1884 First practical fountain pen is made.

1903 Wright brothers make first controlled, sustained flight in a power-driven airplane.

1927 First mechanical television demonstration given to the public.

On Your Own

Use the information in the article to create a second tier for the time line shown.

The Race to Space

During the 1950s and 1960s, both American and Soviet leaders made space exploration an important goal. Both countries wanted to win the space race to show their scientific superiority and military power.

In 1957, the Soviet Union launched *Sputnik*, the first artificial Earth satellite. *Sputnik* means "traveler" in Russian. That same year, the Soviets launched *Sputnik II*. The space craft carried Laika, a dog, into space.

Two years later, in 1959, the Soviet Union launched *Luna II*, the first space probe to hit the moon. That same year, *Luna III* orbited the moon and took photographs of it.

Yuri Gagarin, a Soviet cosmonaut, became the first person to orbit Earth in 1961. And in 1963, the first woman in space was Soviet cosmonaut, Valentina Tereshkova.

The Soviets' accomplishments were impressive and contributed a great deal to what we now know about space.

America's Race to Space

1955
The U.S. launches its first satellite, *Explorer 1*. NASA, the federal agency devoted to space exploration, is formed.

1959
The seven *Mercury* astronauts are selected. U.S. launches two monkeys into space in a Jupiter rocket-nose cone.

1961
Alan Shepard, Jr., becomes the first American astronaut in space.
President Kennedy sets goal of landing an American on the moon by the end of the decade.

1962
John Glenn, Jr., becomes the first American astronaut to orbit Earth.

1968
The U.S. launches the first manned space mission to orbit the moon.

1969
Neil Armstrong, Edwin "Buzz" Aldrin, and Michael Collins are the first astronauts to land on the moon.

1955　1960　1965　1970

The Soviet Union's Race to Space

Sequence

Before You Read

Vocabulary Read the words below. Then match each word or phrase to its clue.

wrestle	clue_____
commercially	clue_____
unique	clue_____
trial and error	clue_____
pivotal	clue_____

What's the Word?

Clue #1: one of a kind
Clue #2: first letter is silent
Clue #3: opposite of "unimportant"
Clue #4: has four syllables
Clue #5: trying until you succeed

As You Read

Text Structure This article gives the **sequence** of important events in the history of flight. To keep track of them, underline the key events. Circle the dates that tell when each event happened.

Text Feature How does the time line help you understand the article?

After You Read

1. Did the first helicopter flight take place before or after the first commercial airplane flight?

2. How many years after the first space flight did *Columbia* orbit Earth?

3. How has air travel changed the way you and people you know live?

A Soaring Century

The invention of the airplane just a little more than 100 years ago changed the world and the way we see ourselves in it.

Taking Off

Last year, more than 8.3 million scheduled flights took off in the United States alone. Airplanes deliver people, mail, and supplies around the world 24 hours a day, 7 days a week. Our economy—our way of life—would be very different if humans had never figured out how to get off the ground.

It's difficult to imagine that just a little more than 100 years ago, the airplane did not exist. People had managed to rise into the air in hot-air balloons. But no one had managed to make a powered flight in a vehicle heavier than air itself.

It wasn't until December 17, 1903, that two brothers from Dayton, Ohio, were finally able to take flight in just such a craft. The year 2003 marked the 100th anniversary of the day that Orville and Wilbur Wright became the first people to successfully pilot an airplane. The first flight took place in Kitty Hawk, North Carolina, lasted 12 seconds, and traveled 120 feet. That short trip would change the course of history.

How They Did It

The Wright brothers fixed bicycles for a living. They loved to wrestle with

1930s First commercial planes are developed. DC-3s are the most common commercial airliners in the mid-1900s.

1939 The first flight of a single-rotor helicopter takes place in the U.S.

1890   1900   1910   **1920**   1930   1940

1903 Orville and Wilbur Wright make the world's first successful airplane flight.

1927 Charles Lindbergh makes the first nonstop solo flight across the Atlantic in the *Spirit of St. Louis.*

1945 Airplanes play a huge role in World War II (1939–1945). A B-29 bomber drops the atomic bomb on Hiroshima, Japan.

mechanical problems. They also knew the value of research. They read everything they could about flight before designing their craft. They learned through trial and error. They had to make several changes to the design of their plane—called the *Flyer*—before they got it right.

The Wright brothers built the *Flyer* from wood and fabric. They chose a **biplane** construction—two wings tied one on top of the other—because of the sturdiness of the design. The brothers then figured out how to make wings that would take advantage of the phenomenon known as **lift**, which helps planes rise into the air.

The Wrights had a unique solution when it came to controlling their vehicle. The brothers took turns flying the plane. They did so by lying down on their stomachs on the bottom wing, and moving their hips from side to side. This movement effectively allowed them to bend one wing or the other, which helped to stabilize the craft in the air. The *Flyer* flew, but without an engine the craft was still just a **glider**. So, the brothers attached a custom-built engine to the *Flyer*, which powered the propellers—and whoosh! The *Flyer* was off. It was the first manned airplane flight.

Revolutionary New Tool

People began flying commercially in the 1930s. Some of the first flights took many, many more hours than they do today. The trip that famed pilot Charles Lindbergh made from the United States to Europe in 1927 took 33.5 hours. Today, flights across the Atlantic Ocean are made in a fraction of that time.

By mid-century, the airplane had also become a powerful wartime tool.

Airplanes became indispensable in battle, beginning in World War II. They were used to transport troops and supplies and to bomb targets. One bombing in particular brought the world into the nuclear age. A B-29 airplane delivered the deadly atomic bomb on Hiroshima, Japan, in 1945. Another atomic bomb was dropped on Nagasaki, Japan, three days later. The blows forced the Japanese to surrender, and began the nuclear standoff of the Cold War years.

Airplanes (and later helicopters) continued to play pivotal roles in subsequent wars. Today, hi-tech fighter jets allow precision hits on targets.

Matter of Pride

Dr. Thomas Crouch is an expert on flight at the Smithsonian National Air and Space Museum in Washington, D.C. He believes that the impact of the Wright brothers' accomplishment is huge.

"Flight came to symbolize the things we all desire, like freedom, and suddenly there were people doing it," Crouch says. "If human beings can figure out how to do that, what can't we do?"

1981 *Columbia*, the first space shuttle to orbit Earth, launches.

1988 The U.S. military unveils the B-2 stealth bomber, with a wingspan the equivalent of half a football field yet undetectable by radar.

50   1960   1970   **1980**   1990   2000   **2010**   2020

1961 Flight takes people into space. The *Vostok* carries Soviet cosmonaut Yuri Gagarin into space, making him the first person to travel there.

2020? Some experts say one day we may literally jet from place to place in helicopter-style air taxis.

Sequence

Reread "A Soaring Century." Fill in the multi-tiered time line with events in the history of flight.

Travel Firsts!

Planes	Dates	Subways
	1880	Boston was the first city to build a subway. Many major cities have followed.
		— 1898 Boston, Massachusetts
1903—	**1900**	
		— 1904 New York, New York
		— 1908 Philadelphia, Pennsylvania
	1920	
1927—		
1930s—		
1939—	**1940**	
		— 1943 Chicago, Illinois
1945—		
		— 1955 Cleveland, Ohio
	1960	
1961—		
		— 1972 San Francisco, California
		— 1976 Washington, D.C.
	1980	
1981—		— 1983 Baltimore, Maryland
		— 1984 Miami, Florida
1988—		
		— 1993 Los Angeles, California
	2000	

Source: U.S. Department of Transportation

 Retell Use the sequence organizer above to retell "A Soaring Century" in your own words. Include as much information as you can remember.

Writing Frame

Use the information in your graphic organizer to fill in the sequence of events in the history of flight in the writing frame.

The history of flight has been long and interesting. The first event in the

history of flight was in _____ when _____

_____.

After that, in _____ Charles Lindbergh _____

_____.

In 1939, _____.

During World War II, _____

_____.

In 1961, _____

_____.

In 1981, _____.

After that, in 1988, _____.

 Use the writing frame above as a model to describe the sequence of events in the development of the light bulb. Look in your science textbook if you need facts that will help you fill in the frame.

LET'S NAVIGATE

Follow the five easy steps when you read nonfiction text.

5 EASY STEPS

Step ① Preview
Read the title, introduction, and headings. Think about what they tell you.

Step ② Prepare
Say to yourself, "This article is going to be about _____. What do I already know?"

Step ③ Read
Carefully read the article.

Step ④ Use the Tools
Stop at special features, such as the special type and the graphics. Ask yourself,

- Why is this here?
- What does it tell me?
- How does it connect to the article?

Step ⑤ Retell/Connect
Retell what you learned. Think about how it connects to your life and the world.

① # THE AMAZING OCTOPUS

The octopus is an awesome ocean animal. It can be as HUGE as 30 feet or as tiny as 1 inch in length. What makes this creature so amazing?

Body Parts

③ An octopus has 8 arms that it uses to swim and to catch food. An octopus has suction cups on the back of its arms.

④ **Suction cups** help the octopus grab a meal, such as crabs, clams, and fish. If an octopus loses an arm, it can grow another one. This is called **regeneration** (ree-gen-uh-RAY-shun). A starfish can do the same thing.

An octopus has no bones, so its body is soft and squishy. This allows it to squeeze into small spaces. An octopus can squeeze into a seashell! This helps the octopus chase food even into little cracks.

Survival Skills ②

Octopuses have many ways to avoid their enemies. An octopus can change colors as **camouflage** (KAM-uh-flahzh), a way to blend in with its surroundings. That way, its enemies can't see it. And, in the blink of an eye, it can make its skin bumpy. To an enemy, the octopus looks like just another rock!

An octopus can also squirt purple-black ink at its enemies. The enemy can't see the octopus through the ink, and the octopus can quickly swim away to safety.

SCHOLASTIC
TEXT STRUCTURES

Cause/ Effect

cause → effect

Problem/ Solution

problem → solution

Sequence

step 1 step 2 step 3 step 4

Description

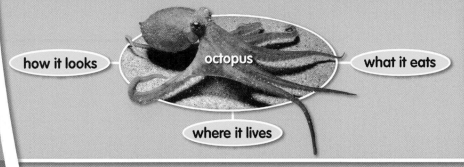

how it looks   octopus   what it eats

where it lives

Compare/ Contrast

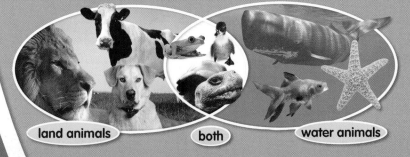

land animals   both   water animals

Sequence

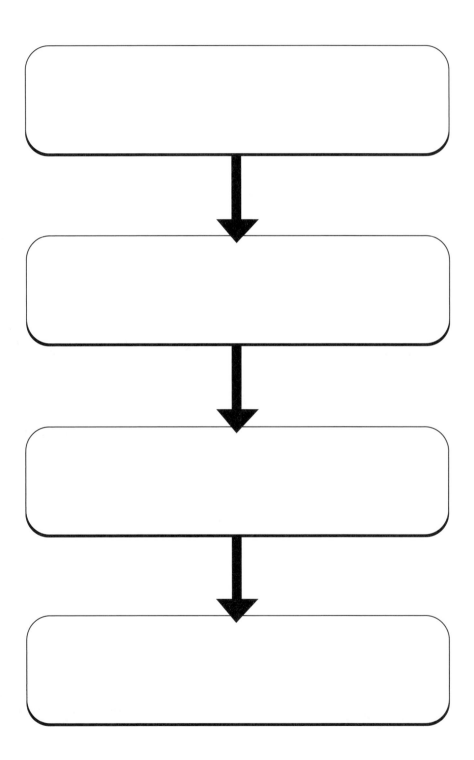

Compare/Contrast

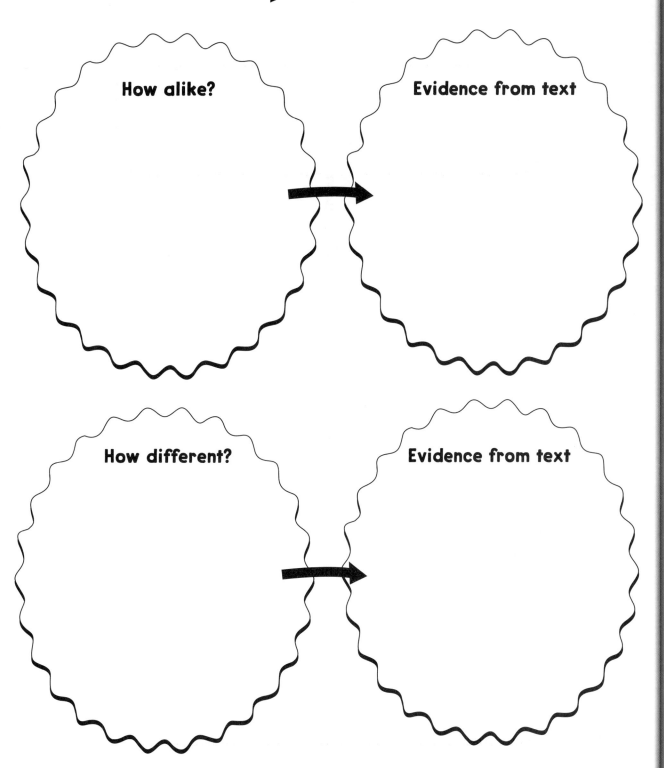

How alike?

Evidence from text

How different?

Evidence from text

Cause/Effect

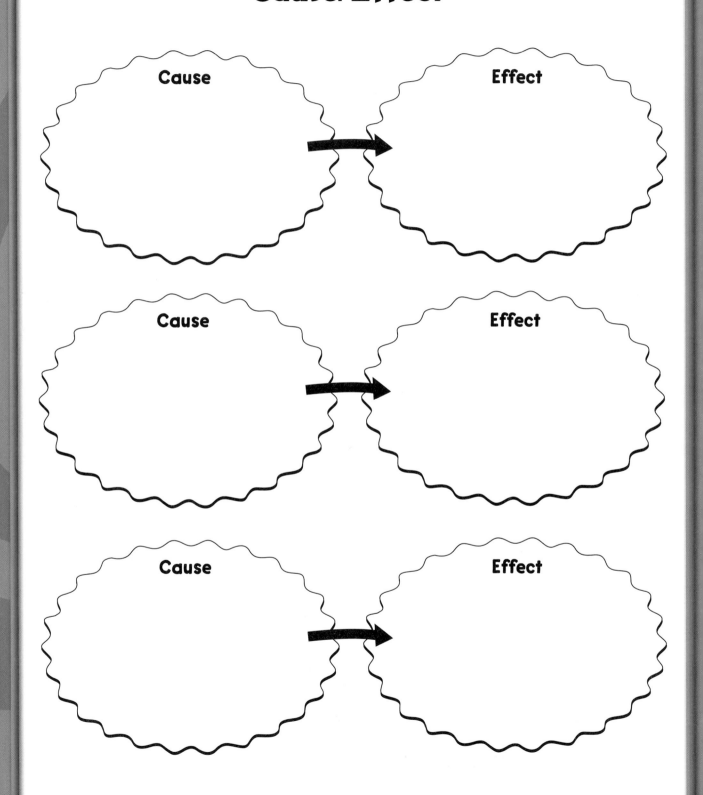

Cause

Effect

Cause

Effect

Cause

Effect

Problem/Solution

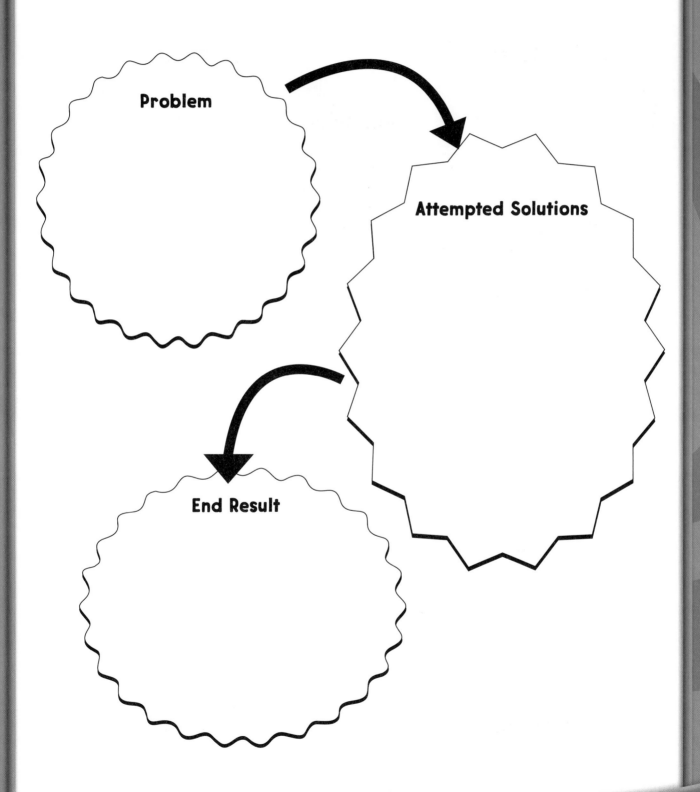

Problem

Attempted Solutions

End Result

Description

Main Idea _____

_____

Detail 1 _____

_____

Detail 2 _____

_____

Detail 3 _____

_____

Detail 4 _____

_____

Credits

Text: "Nature's Fury," "A Dog's Life," "Dealing With Dollars," "Race Against the Clock," "Wild Winds," "Ancient Writing Discovery," "Skin and Bones," "Welcome to America," "Fighting Off Food Allergies," "Peanuts: Public Enemy Number 1?," "Breaking Barriers," "La Causa," "Mmmm . . . Chocolate," "Ice in Space," "Eye of the 'Tiger'," "Amazing Inventors," "Secret Code of Battle," "Creatures of the Deep," "Bats of the World," "Bat Buddy," "All Snowed Inn," "Dancing With Pride," "Consumer Sales," "The Life of a $ Bill," "Kids' Money," "A Real Education in Money," "Angels of the Animal ER," "The White House Turned 200!," "Civil War Treasure Is Shipshape," "Standing Tall," "A New World," "Arctic Region," "Preserving a Proud Past," "Building the Capital," "A Soaring Century," are reprinted from SCHOLASTIC NEWS. Copyright © 1998, 2000, 2001, 2002, 2003, 2004, 2005 by Scholastic Inc. Reprinted by permission. "Journey Into the Earth," "Earth's Gooey Cave Creatures," "Dirt," "This National Park Could Explode!," "Secrets of a Supercolony," "Croc Chasers," and "Attack on the Titanic!" are reprinted from SUPER SCIENCE. Copyright © 2002, 2003, 2004, 2005 by Scholastic Inc. Reprinted by permission. "The Melba Pattillo Story" is reprinted from www.scholastic.com. Copyright © 2006–1996. Reprinted by permission. "How Footballs Are Made" is reprinted from MY FIRST BOOK OF HOW THINGS ARE MADE. Copyright © 1998 by Scholastic Inc. Reprinted by permission. "Getting Your Homework Done" is reprinted from SCHOLASTIC CHOICES. Copyright © 2000 by Scholastic Inc. Reprinted by permission. Artifact descriptions and letter from The Mariners' Museum, Newport News, Virginia. "Sequoyah and the Cherokee" is reprinted from REGIONS: ADVENTURES IN TIME AND SPACE. Copyright © 1997 by Macmillan/McGraw-Hill. Reprinted by permission. "Blizzard Warning" is reprinted from TEACHING STUDENTS TO READ NONFICTION. Copyright © 2003 by Alice Boynton and Wiley Blevins, published by Scholastic Inc. Reprinted by permission. "Ben Franklin, Scientist and Inventor" and "Time for Inventions" are from AMERICAN HISTORY TIME LINES. Copyright © 1996 by Susan Washburn Buckley, published by Scholastic Inc.

Images: Cover: Ink anemone fish © David Fleetham/Getty Images; Money © A.Huber/U.Starke/Zefa/Corbis; Girl and dog © Corbis RF/Jupiter Images; Capitol building DC © Peter Gridley/Getty Images. Page 4: (from top) Sayyid Azim/AP Images; Brian LaRossa. Page 5: (from top) Chris Collins/Corbis; Mapman/Scholastic. Page 7: Corbis. Page 8: (from top left, clockwise) Royalty-Free/Corbis; Royalty-Free/Corbis; © Tim Pannell/Corbis; © LWA-JDC/Corbis. Page 10: Rusty Russell/Getty. Page 11: Brian LaRossa. Page 14: (from left) © Enzo & Paolo Ragazzini/Corbis; Brian LaRossa. Page 15: North Wind Picture Archives. Page 16: © Mathers Museum of World Cultures, Bloomington, IN. Page 17: (from left) © Gregory Wenzel/Judith River Dinosaur Institute; © Mark Thompson/ Judith River Dinosaur Institute. Page 18: (from top) Michael Nichols/National Geographic Image Collection; Michael Nichols/ National Geographic Image Collection. Page 19: © Kenneth Ingham. Page 20: (bottom) Library of Congress. Page 21: (top) Altrendo Images; (bottom, from left) Dorothea Lange; Collection of George Eastman House; Sander/Gamma Liaison. Page 24: A. Syred/Photo Researchers, Inc. Page 25: (milk/soy) Brian LaRossa; (all others) Copyright © 2007 Scholastic and its licensors. Page 27: AP World Wide Photo. Page 28: (from top) Jocelyn Sherman/Courtesy of Cesar Chavez Foundation; © Bettmann/Corbis. Page 30: (from top) Greg Pease/Getty Images; Owen Franken/Corbis; Greg Pease/Getty Images. Page 31: (top) Ron Giling/Peter Arnold; (bottom, from left) Scott Camazine/PhotoResearchers, Inc.; Nigel J.H. Smith/Animals Animals. Page 34: (from left) © Lester Lefkowitz/Corbis; Brian LaRossa. Page 35: (from top) NASA and G. Bacon; (illustration) Brian LaRossa. Page 36–37: Peter Bollinger. Page 38: Courtesy of Wilson Sporting Goods Co. Page 40: (from left) Christian Koenig; C.C. Lockwood/Animals Animals; (map) Mapman/Scholastic. Page 41: 5W Infographics. Page 45: Jeremy Woodhouse/Masterfile. Page 47: (top, from left) Ateila Bundles/Walker Family Collection; Courtesy of Christine Donovan; Courtesy of Gihon Foundation; (bottom, from left) Scholastic Inc.; Photodisc; Index Stock. Page 48: (from top) Courtesy of the Code Book/Doubleday; Monica Almeida/NYT Pictures. Page 50: (from left) Pete Atkinson/Getty Images; Villoch-Visual & Written/Bruce Coleman Inc. Page 51: (from top) Courtesy of ABP Environment Ocean London; Courtesy of Bill Eschmeyer & John E. Randall/Census of Marine Life. Page 54: (clockwise, from top) B & B Wells/Animals Animals; M.W. Larso/Bruce Coleman; Dr. Merlin D. Tuttle/Photo Researchers; (illustration) Jason Robinson. Page 55: (top & middle) Courtesy of Bat World Sanctuary; Robert & Linda Mitchell. Page 56: Dr. Merlin D. Tuttle/Photo Researchers. Page 57: (from left) © Layne Kennedy/Corbis; © Poulin Pierre Paul/Corbis Sygma. Page 58: Kent Meireis/The Image Works. Page 59: Courtesy American Indian Culture Research Center, Blue Cloud Abbey, Marvin, South Dakota. Page 60: (from top) Shaen Adey/ABPL/Animals Animals; © Martin Harvery/NHPA. Page 61: © F. Stuart Westmorland/Photo Researchers; Copyright © John Gerlach/Animals Animals/Earth Scenes; © W. Treat Davidson/Photo Researchers. Page 64: Brian LaRossa. Page 65: (top) © Laura Pedrick/Getty Images for Scholastic. Page 67: Brian LaRossa. Page 68: (top) The Republic Photo; (iguana) JC Carton/Bruce Coleman Inc; (bottom) Courtesy of the MSPCA— Angell Animal Medical Center. Page 70: Courtesy John and Jan Zweifel Family, Orlando, FL. Page 74: (from top) Courtesy NOAA; © 2002 Getty Images/Newscom. Page 75: © Bettmann/Corbis. Page 76: (clockwise, from left) © Philip Gould/Corbis; © David Muench/Corbis; James L. Amos/Corbis. Page 77: (from left) © Bettmann/Corbis; Courtesy USPS. Page 78: New York Historical

Society. Page 79: © Bettmann/Corbis. Page 80: (Ballard) Christopher W. Morrow/Photo Researchers, Inc. Page 81: (bottom left) SPL/Photo Researchers, Inc; (map) Mapman/Scholastic; (chart) Jim McMahon, Source USA Today. Page 84: (from left) © Steven E. Sutton/Duomo/Corbis; © Max Morse/Reuters/Corbis; (map) Brian LaRossa. Page 85: (from top) © 2003 Michael Pilla/Getty; Brian LaRossa. Page 86: Brian LaRossa. Page 87: (from left) Dan Guravich/Corbis; Brian LaRossa. Page 88: (clockwise, from top left) © Royalty-Free/Corbis; © Konrad Wothe/Oxford Scientific; © Jose Fuste Raga/Corbis; © Galen Rowell/Corbis; © Angelo Cavalli/Zefa/Corbis; © Rob Howard/Corbis; (map) Brian LaRossa. Page 89–90: Brian LaRossa. Page 91: (from top) © Karen Baldwin; Jason Robinson. Page 94: © Bernard Annebicque/Corbis Sygma. Page 97: (from left) © Bettmann/Corbis; Courtesy of Independence National Historic Park via SODA. Page 98: Teresa Southwell. Page 100: Peter Bollinger. Page 101: (clockwise, from top left) NASA; © Aero Graphics, Inc./Corbis; Peter Bollinger; © Bettmann/Corbis. Page 104: (from top) David Fleetham/Pacific Stock; © Mark Conlin/SeaPics.com; Eiichi Korasawa/Photo Researchers. Page 105: (from left to right) © Paul & Lindamarie Ambrose/Getty Images; © Albany Herald/Corbis Sygma; © Josef Beck/Getty Images; © Creatas/Jupiter Images; © Jim Zipp/Photo Researchers; © Jane Burton/Nature Picture Library; © Jef Meul/Foto Natura/Minden Pictures; © George McCarthy/Corbis; © Mark Conlin/SeaPics.com; © DLILLC/Corbis; © Brian Brown/Getty Images; © Tim McGuire/Corbis; © Royalty-Free/Corbis; © Martin Harvey/Corbis; © Gavriel Jecan/Corbis; © Denis Scott/Corbis; © Royalty-Free/Corbis; © Georgette Douwma/Getty Images.

Every effort has been made to acquire credit information for and permission to use the materials in this book.

Editor: Mela Ottaiano
Cover Design: Jorge J. Namerow